Praise for Zbigniew Brzezinski's *Strategic Vision*

"When it comes to offering a vision to guide American foreign policy, Zbigniew Brzezinski's latest book, unlike so much other literature of this type, refuses to lament or exaggerate the alleged decline in American power and influence. . . . [A] welcome antidote to the dreary school of 'declinism' now dominating much of the foreign-policy conversation."

—*The New Republic*

"In his *New York Times* best-seller, *Strategic Vision*, Zbigniew Brzezinski provides a desperately needed wake-up call to America's political and business leaders as the world's center of gravity shifts from the West to the East."

—*Ventura County Star*

"Brzezinski's book is foremost a wake-up call for America's political elites. . . . Brzezinski's analysis about the challenges to US primacy and broader international stability is as sharp as always. . . . This book makes an excellent case for why US leadership remains essential in an ever-complex world."

—*Rusi Journal*

"*Strategic Vision* provides a very straightforward and candid assessment of the role of America in the international arena as well as an insightful strategy for America to maintain its irreplaceable leadership in the short and medium terms, making the book a must-read for anyone in the United States foreign policy field. . . . Brzezinski presents a masterfully written . . . vision for the future of geopolitics and America's role in the world."

—*e-International Relations* (online)

"This new book deserves attention because it seems written by a mind in agony about the world's future."

—*The Spokesman* (UK)

"Once again, Brzezinski gives the reader thoughtful insight on the state of global affairs and America's place in the world. He provides a wakeup call to international affairs and their effect on this country."

—*Polish American Journal*

"The central message of *Strategic Vision* is how much more ghastly it will be on all fronts if America cannot urgently mobilize a national will for renewal."

—*Daily Beast*

"This short book, crammed with facts and acute analysis, well presents Zbigniew Brzezinski's considered 'strategic vision' of the future world and the changed but still vital leadership role of the United States."

—*Michigan War Studies Review*

"*Strategic Vision* is a powerful documentation of the steps that must be taken to ensure continued American success."

—*Midwest Book Review*

"Rigorous and insightful analysis. . . . [Brzezinski's] *realpolitik* approach . . . is actually refreshing in today's age of flippant air-bombing humanitarianism."

—*Spiked Review of Books* (online)

"Zbigniew Brzezinski . . . has written another important book."

—*The Diplomat* (Asia)

"[Brzezinski] puts forth a strong vision in his 200-page book. Politicians like German Chancellor Angela Merkel and French President Nicolas Sarkozy should read it."

—*Today's Zaman* (Turkey)

"[Brzezinski] offers an astute, elegant appraisal of the waning of America's 'global appeal' and the severe consequences of the shifting of power from West to East. . . . Brzezinski provides a powerful cautionary tale. . . . An urgent call for 'historic renewal' by one of America's sharpest minds."

—*Kirkus Reviews*

STRATEGIC VISION

—Also by Zbigniew Brzezinski —

America and the World

Second Chance

The Choice

The Geostrategic Triad

The Grand Chessboard

Out of Control

The Grand Failure

In Quest of National Security

Game Plan

Power and Principle

Between Two Ages

Alternative to Partition

The Soviet Bloc

Totalitarian Dictatorship and Autocracy

The Permanent Purge

STRATEGIC VISION

America and the Crisis of Global Power

Zbigniew Brzezinski

BASIC BOOKS
A MEMBER OF THE PERSEUS BOOKS GROUP
New York

Hardcover first published in 2012 by Basic Books,
A Member of the Perseus Books Group
Paperback first published in 2013 by Basic Books

The Library of Congress has cataloged the hardcover as follows:
Brzezinski, Zbigniew, 1928-
Strategic vision : America and the crisis of global power / Zbigniew Brzezinski.
p. cm.
Includes index.
ISBN 978-0-465-02954-9 (hardcover : alk. paper) —
ISBN 978-0-465-02955-6 (ebook) 1. Balance of power—Forecasting. 2. International relations—History—21st century—Forecasting. 3. United States—Foreign relations—21st century—Forecasting. 4. World politics—21st century—Forecasting. 5. Geopolitics—History—21st century—Forecasting. I. Title.
JZ1313.B79 2012
327.1'12—dc23
2011033312

ISBN 978-0-465-06181-5 (paperback)

10 9 8 7 6 5 4 3 2 1

CONTENTS

LIST OF MAPS AND FIGURES

Figures

Maps

Introduction

THE WORLD IS NOW INTERACTIVE AND INTERDEPENDENT. IT IS ALSO, for the first time, a world in which the problems of human survival have begun to overshadow more traditional international conflicts. Unfortunately, the major powers have yet to undertake globally cooperative responses to the new and increasingly grave challenges to human well-being—environmental, climatic, socioeconomic, nutritional, or demographic. And without basic geopolitical stability, any effort to achieve the necessary global cooperation will falter.

Indeed, the changing distribution of global power and the new phenomenon of massive political awakening intensify, each in its own way, the volatility of contemporary international relations. As China's influence grows and as other emerging powers—Russia or India or Brazil for example—compete with each other for resources, security, and economic advantage, the potential for miscalculation and conflict increases. Accordingly, the United States must seek to shape a broader geopolitical foundation for constructive cooperation in the global arena, while accommodating the rising aspirations of an increasingly restless global population.

With the foregoing in mind, this book seeks to respond to four major questions:

1. What are the implications of the changing distribution of global power from the West to the East, and how is it being affected by the new reality of a politically awakened humanity?
2. Why is America's global appeal waning, what are the symptoms of America's domestic and international decline, and how did America waste the unique global opportunity offered by the peaceful end of the Cold War? Conversely, what are America's recuperative strengths and what geopolitical reorientation is necessary to revitalize America's world role?
3. What would be the likely geopolitical consequences *if* America declined from its globally preeminent position, who would be the almost-immediate geopolitical victims of such a decline, what effects would it have on the global-scale problems of the twenty-first century, and could China assume America's central role in world affairs by 2025?
4. Looking beyond 2025, how should a resurgent America define its long-term geopolitical goals, and how could America, with its traditional European allies, seek to engage Turkey and Russia in order to construct an even larger and more vigorous West? Simultaneously, how could America achieve balance in the East between the need for close cooperation with China and the fact that a constructive American role in Asia should be neither exclusively China-centric nor involve dangerous entanglements in Asian conflicts?

In answering these questions this book will argue that America's role in the world will continue to be essential in the years to come. Indeed, the ongoing changes in the distribution of global power and mounting global strife make it all the more imperative that America not retreat into an ignorant garrison-state mentality or wallow in self-righteous cultural hedonism. Such an America could cause the geopolitical prospects of an evolving world—in which the center of gravity is shifting from West to East—to become increasingly grave. The world needs an America that is economically vital, socially appealing, responsibly powerful, strategically deliberate, internationally respected, and historically enlightened in its global engagement with the new East.

How likely is such a globally purposeful America? Today, America's historical mood is uneasy, and notions of America's decline as historically inevitable are intellectually fashionable. However, this kind of periodic pessimism is neither novel nor self-fulfilling. Even the belief that the twentieth century was "America's century," which became widespread in the wake of World War II, did not preclude phases of anxiety regarding America's long-range future.

When the Soviet Union launched Sputnik, its first orbital satellite, during the Eisenhower administration, Americans became concerned about their prospects in both peaceful competition and strategic warfare. And again, when the United States failed to achieve a meaningful victory in Vietnam during the Nixon years, Soviet leaders confidently predicted America's demise while historically pessimistic American policy makers sought détente in exchange for the status quo in the divided Europe. But America proved to be more resilient and the Soviet system eventually imploded.

By 1991, following the disintegration both of the Soviet bloc and then the Soviet Union itself, the United States was left standing as the only global superpower. Not only the twentieth but even the twenty-first century then seemed destined to be the American centuries. Both President Bill Clinton and President George W. Bush confidently asserted as much. And academic circles echoed them with bold prognoses that the end of the Cold War meant in effect "the end of history" insofar as doctrinal debates regarding the relative superiority of competing social systems was concerned. The victory of liberal democracy was proclaimed not only as decisive but also as final. Given that liberal democracy had flowered first in the West, the implied assumption was that henceforth the West would be the defining standard for the world.

However, such super-optimism did not last long. The culture of self-gratification and deregulation that began during the Clinton years and continued under President George W. Bush led to the bursting of one stock market bubble at the turn of the century and a full-scale financial crash less than a decade later. The costly unilateralism of the younger Bush presidency led to a decade of war in the Middle East and the derailment of American foreign policy at large. The financial catastrophe of 2008 nearly precipitated a calamitous economic depression, jolting America and much of the West into a sudden recognition of their systemic vulnerability to unregulated greed. Moreover, in China and other Asian states a perplexing amalgam of economic liberalism and state capitalism demonstrated a surprising capacity for economic growth and technological innovation. This in turn prompted new anxiety about the future of America's status as the leading world power.

Indeed, there are several alarming similarities between the Soviet Union in the years just prior to its fall and the America of the early twenty-first century. The Soviet Union, with an increasingly gridlocked governmental system incapable of enacting serious policy revisions, in effect bankrupted itself by committing an inordinate percentage of its GNP to a decades-long military rivalry with the United States and exacerbated this problem by taking on the additional costs of a decade-long attempt to conquer Afghanistan. Not surprisingly, it could not afford to sustain its competition with America in cutting-edge technological sectors and thus fell further behind; its economy stumbled and the society's quality of life further deteriorated in comparison to the West; its ruling Communist class became cynically insensitive to widening social disparities while hypocritically masking its own privileged life-style; and finally, in foreign affairs it became increasingly self-isolated, while precipitating a geopolitically damaging hostility with its once-prime Eurasian ally, Communist China.

These parallels, even if overdrawn, fortify the case that America must renew itself and pursue a comprehensive and long-term geopolitical vision, one that is responsive to the challenges of the changing historical context. Only a dynamic and strategically minded America, together with a unifying Europe, can jointly promote a larger and more vital

West, one capable of acting as a responsible partner to the rising and increasingly assertive East. Otherwise, a geopolitically divided and self-centered West could slide into a historical decline reminiscent of the humiliating impotence of nineteenth-century China, while the East might be tempted to replicate the self-destructive power rivalries of twentieth-century Europe.

In brief, the crisis of global power is the cumulative consequence of the dynamic shift in the world's center of gravity from the West to the East, of the accelerated surfacing of the restless phenomenon of global political awakening, and of America's deficient domestic and international performance since its emergence by 1990 as the world's only superpower. The foregoing poses serious longer-term risks to the survival of some endangered states, to the security of the global commons, and to global stability at large. This book seeks to outline the needed strategic vision, looking beyond 2025.

Zbigniew Brzezinski
March 2011

- PART I -

The Receding West

In the long run, global politics are bound to become increasingly uncongenial to the concentration of hegemonic power in the hands of a single state. Hence, America is not only the first, as well as the only, truly global superpower, but it is also likely to be the very last. . . .

Economic power is also likely to become more dispersed. In the years to come, no single power is likely to reach the level of 30 percent or so of the world's GDP that America sustained throughout much of this century, not to speak of the 50 percent at which it crested in 1945.

—FROM CONCLUSION TO *The Grand Chessboard*, BY THIS AUTHOR, 1997, P. 210

THE LONG-LASTING POLITICAL DOMINATION OF THE WORLD BY THE West has been fading for some decades. For a brief moment in the 1990s, however, it looked as if the West, despite Europe's twin attempts at collective suicide during the first half of the twentieth century, might stage a historical comeback. The peaceful end of the Cold War, culminating in the fragmentation of the Soviet Union, signaled the final step in the rapid ascendance of the United States as the first truly global superpower. That internationally dominant power, together with its politically motivated and economically dynamic partner, the European Union, appeared capable not only of reviving the West's global preeminence but also of defining for itself a constructive global role.

Twenty years later, few expect the European Union to emerge soon as a politically serious global player while America's preeminent global status seems tenuous. Because the West as a whole is now less capable of acting in unison, its lasting political legacy is thus also more in doubt. Once upon a time, though briefly, it did seem that worldwide democracy, international peace, and increasingly even a comfortable social compact would be the West's enduring bequest to humanity. However, basic changes in the distribution of global power, the impact of the new phenomenon of global political awakening on the exercise of that power, and the negative consequences of recent US foreign policy moves and of growing doubts regarding the vitality of the American system have cumulatively put that more hopeful legacy of the West in question.

1: The Emergence of Global Power

The very notion of a globally dominant power is a recent historical development. For millennia, people lived in isolated communities, unaware of the existence of their more distant neighbors. Migrations and sporadic collisions with outsiders took place in a setting of total ignorance of the world at large. It has only been within the last eight hundred years or so that an initially vague awareness of the presence of distant "others" permeated the human consciousness, first through expeditions and mapping of once-unknown areas and then through colonization and large migrations. Eventually, that knowledge led to imperial rivalries, which in turn led to two destructive wars for world domination, and then to the global systemic confrontation of the Cold War. In recent times, space exploration has dramatized the new appreciation of the relative "smallness" of the earth, while photographs from outer space taken at night have conveyed the vivid contrast between the illuminated concentrations of urbanized humanity—especially in what is usually described as the West—and the darker, less

MAP 1.1 THE EARTH AT NIGHT

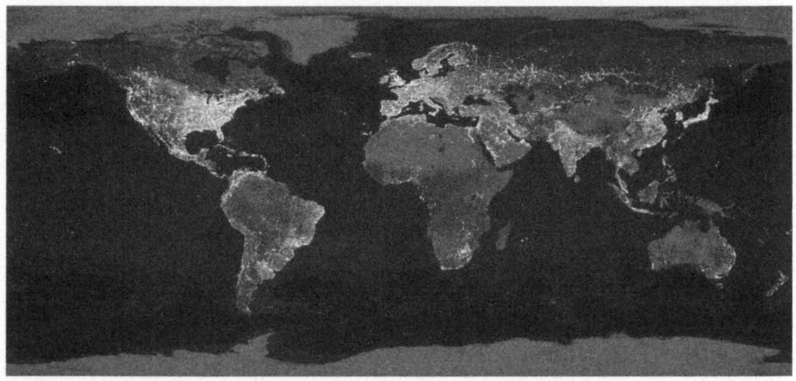

technologically advanced, but increasingly crowded regions of the rest of the world.

The states located on the Western European shores of the North Atlantic Ocean were the first to set out, self-consciously and vigorously, on the world at large. They were driven by a potent mix of maritime technological advancement, proselytizing passion, visions of monarchical and personal glory, and out-and-out material greed. Partially as a result of this head start, they controlled territory far away from their continental home bases for nearly half a millennium. The geographic scope of the West thus expanded—first by conquest and then by settlement—from Europe's Atlantic shores to the Western Hemisphere. Portugal and Spain conquered and colonized South America while Britain and France did the same in North America. Eventual political independence from Europe by both Americas was then followed by large-scale European migration into the Western Hemisphere. In the meantime, the Western European maritime states bordering on the Atlantic also reached into the Indian and Pacific Oceans, establishing dominion over today's India and Indonesia, imposing a patronizing presence in parts of China, carving up almost all of Africa and the Middle East, and seizing scores of islands in the Pacific and Indian Oceans as well as in the Caribbean Sea.

EMPIRES AT THEIR GREATEST EXTENT

1.	British Empire (1920)	34,000,000 km^2
2.	Mongol Empire (1309)	24,000,000 km^2
3.	Russian Empire (1905)	23,000,000 km^2
4.	Second French Colonial Empire (1920)	15,000,000 km^2
5.	Manchu-Qing Dynasty, China (1800)	15,000,000 km^2
6.	Spanish Empire (1800)	14,000,000 km^2
7.	Umayyad Caliphate (720)	11,000,000 km^2
8.	Yuan Dynasty, China (1320)	11,000,000 km^2
9.	Abbasid Caliphate (750)	11,000,000 km^2
10.	Portuguese Empire (1815)	10,400,000 km^2
11.	Achaemenid Empire, Persia (480 BC)	8,000,000 km^2
12.	Roman Empire (117)	6,500,000 km^2

From the sixteenth century until the midpoint of the twentieth, this combination of cultural and political outreach made the European states of the North Atlantic politically dominant in areas spanning the globe. (In that respect, their imperial domains differed fundamentally from the much earlier but essentially isolated and contiguous regional empires—such as the Roman, Persian, Mughal, Mongol, Chinese, or Incan—each of which conceived of itself as the center of the world but with little geographic knowledge of the world beyond.) Tsarist Russia massively expanded its land-based empire from the seventeenth through the nineteenth centuries, but it similarly absorbed only adjoining territory with the brief exception of Alaska. The same was true of the Ottoman Empire's expansion in the Middle East and Southeast Europe.

But while the European maritime powers on the Atlantic Coast ranged over the world, the prolonged conflicts among them weakened their geopolitical position relative to rising powers from within the European continent and from North America. The material and strategic cost of prolonged war in the Low Countries and German provinces during the sixteenth and seventeenth centuries exhausted Iberian power, while Dutch prominence began to wane during the late seventeenth century in the face of ascending Britain on the seas and assertive France next door on land. By the time the smoke cleared in the mid-eighteenth century, Great Britain and France stood as the only remaining competitors in the struggle for imperial dominance.

Their transoceanic rivalry for colonial possessions expanded during the nineteenth century into a contest for supremacy over Europe itself, before turning early in the twentieth century into a joint alliance against a rising European continental power that not coincidentally also had entered the global colonial competition—Germany. From the consequent two world wars, Europe emerged devastated, divided, and demoralized. Indeed, after 1945 a vast Eurasian land power, the Soviet Union, victoriously ensconced in Europe's geographic middle, seemed poised—like the Mongol Empire some seven hundred years earlier—to sweep even further westward.

Meanwhile, across the North Atlantic, the United States spent the nineteenth century developing its industrial and military capabilities in felicitous geographic isolation from the devastating continental and imperial rivalries of Europe. Its interventions in the two world wars of the first half of the twentieth century were decisive in preventing the preponderance of German power in Europe, and it did so while shielded from the unprecedented destruction and carnage of those conflicts. Moreover, America's enviable economic and geopolitical position at the end of World War II hoisted upon it a novel status—one of global preeminence. As a result, the subsequent American-Soviet Cold War precipitated the emergence of a redefined cross-Atlantic West, one dependent on and therefore dominated by the United States of America.

America and the independent western remnants of Europe—bonded by the common goal of containing Soviet Russia as well as by similar political and economic systems and therefore ideological orientations—became the geopolitical core of the newly delineated Atlantic world, defensively preoccupied with its own survival in the face of the trans-Eurasian Sino-Soviet bloc. That bond was institutionalized in the realm of security with the creation of the transoceanic NATO, while Western Europe, seeking to accelerate its postwar recovery, integrated economically through the adoption of the European Economic Community, which later evolved into the European Union. But, still vulnerable to Soviet power, Western Europe became almost formally America's protectorate and informally its economic-financial dependency.

Within four or so decades, however, that same cross-Atlantic and defensive West emerged suddenly as the globally dominant West. The implosion in 1991 of the Soviet Union—in the wake of the fragmentation two years earlier of the Soviet bloc in Eastern Europe—was caused by a combination of social fatigue, political ineptitude, the ideological and economic failings of Marxism, and the successful Western foreign policies of military containment and peaceful ideological penetration. Its immediate consequence was the end of Europe's half-century-long division. Globally, it also highlighted the emergence of the European Union as a major financial and economic (and potentially perhaps even military/political) powerhouse in its own right. Thus, with the unifying Europe still geopolitically wedded to the United States—by then the world's only military superpower as well as the world's most innovative and richest economy—the Atlantic West on the eve of the twenty-first century seemed poised for a new era of Western global supremacy.

The financial and economic framework for that global supremacy already existed. Even during the Cold War, the Atlantic West, due to its capitalist system and the extraordinary dynamism of the American economy, had a clear financial and economic advantage over its geopolitical and ideological antagonist, the Soviet Union. Consequently, despite facing serious military threats, the Atlantic powers were able to institutionalize their dominant position in global affairs through an emerging network of cooperative international organizations, ranging from the World Bank and the IMF to the UN itself, thus seemingly consolidating a global framework for their enduring preeminence.

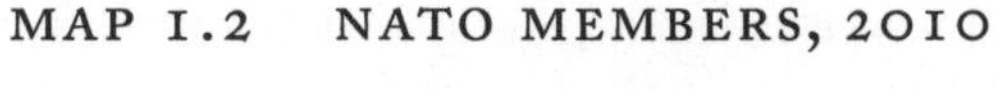

MAP 1.2 NATO MEMBERS, 2010

The West's ideological appeal rose similarly during this period. In Central and Eastern Europe, the West was able to project its appealing vision of human rights and political freedom, thus putting the Soviet Union on the ideological defensive. By the end of the Cold War, America and the Western world found themselves generally associated with the globally attractive principles of human dignity, freedom, and prosperity.

Nonetheless, while the resulting appeal of the West was greater than ever, its geographic scope of control had actually shrunk in the immediate aftermath of World War II. The Western imperial powers had emerged from the two world wars profoundly weakened, while the newly dominant America repudiated the imperial legacy of its European allies. President Roosevelt made no secret of his conviction that the US commitment to the liberation of Europe during World War II did not include the restoration of the colonial empires of Great Britain, France, the Netherlands, Belgium, or Portugal.

However, Roosevelt's highly principled opposition to colonialism did not prevent him from pursuing an acquisitive US policy determined to gain a lucrative position for America in the key oil-producing Middle Eastern countries. In 1943, President Roosevelt not so subtly told Britain's ambassador to the United States, Lord Halifax, while pointing at a map of the Middle East, that "Persian oil is yours. We share the oil of Iraq and Kuwait. As for Saudi Arabian oil, it's ours."[1] So began America's subsequently painful political involvement in that region.

The end of the European empires was even more so the product of the growing restlessness of their colonial subjects. National emancipation became their battle cry, while Soviet ideological and even military support made repression too costly. The new political reality was that the dissolution of the old colonial empires of the European-centric West was unavoidable. The British wisely withdrew—before being forcefully challenged to do so—from India and later from the Middle East (though they left behind religious and ethnic violence that produced a colossal human tragedy in India and an intractable Israeli-Palestinian political conflict that still haunts the West in the Middle East). With US encouragement, they then made a semivoluntary withdrawal from their colonies in Africa. The Dutch in the East Indies (Indonesia) chose to stay and fight—and lost. So did the French in two bloody colonial wars fought first in Vietnam and then in Algeria. The Portuguese withdrew under pressure from Mozambique and Angola. The West's geographic scope thus shrank even as its geopolitical and economic preeminence rose, largely due to the expanding global reach of America's cultural, economic, and political power.

At the same time—obscured from public awareness by the fog of the Cold War—a more basic shift in the global distribution of political and economic power was also taking place. Eventually, it gave birth to a new pecking order in the international system, seen more clearly for the first time as a consequence of the financial crisis of late 2007. This crisis made clear that coping with global economic challenges now required the strength not just of the world's only superpower, or of the West as a whole, but also of the states that hitherto had been considered not yet qualified to take part in global financial-economic decision making.

The practical acceptance of this new reality came with the 2008 admission of new entrants from Asia, Africa, and Latin America into the G-8, a hitherto exclusive and largely Western club of financial decision makers, transforming its previously narrow circle into the more globally representative G-20. Symbolic of this change was the fact that the most significant leadership roles in the first G-20 meeting held in the United States in 2009 were played by the presidents of two states: the United States of America and the People's Republic of China, respectively.

The cumulative effect of these events was to make self-evident a new geopolitical reality: the consequential shift in the center of gravity of global power and of economic dynamism from the Atlantic toward the Pacific, from the West toward the East. To be sure, economic historians remind us that in fact Asia had been the predominant producer of the world's total GNP for some eighteen centuries. As late as the year 1800, Asia accounted for about 60% of the world's total GNP, in contrast to Europe's 30%. India's share alone of the global product in 1750 amounted to 25% (according to Jaswant Singh, former Indian finance minister), much like that of the United States today. But during the nineteenth and twentieth centuries, with the intrusion of European imperialism backed by Europe's surging industrial innovation and financial sophistication, Asia's global share declined precipitously. By 1900, for example, under prolonged British imperial rule, India's share shrank to a mere 1.6%.

In China, just as in India, British imperialism followed in the wake of British traders. The latter had run up huge monetary deficits by purchasing Chinese tea, porcelain, silk, and so on, for which they sought remedy by selling opium to Chinese importers. Beijing's belated efforts to ban the import of opium and restrict the access of foreign merchants then precipitated two armed interventions, first by the British and then by both the British and the French, which further contributed to a precipitous decline in China's role in the global economy.

The historic fact of China's and India's past economic preeminence has led some to argue that the current economic rise of Asia is basically a return to a distant but prolonged normality. But it is important to note that Asia's earlier superiority in GNP was attained in a world of basically isolated regions and thus of very limited economic interactions. The economic links between Europe and Asia involved trade based largely on barter, transacted primarily in just a few ports (notably Calcutta) or transported by periodic caravans slowly traversing the Silk Route. A global economy, continuously interactive and increasingly interdependent, did not then exist.

Thus, in times past, Asia's statistically impressive but isolated economic prowess was not projected outward. In the early part of the fifteenth century, China chose a policy of vigorously enforced self-isolation, having even earlier refrained from exploiting the technological superiority of its commercial fleet and oceanic navy to assert a political outreach. India under the Mughal Empire possessed great wealth, but it lacked political cohesion or external ambitions. Indeed, the only significant case of assertive westward projection of Asian political power occurred under the leadership of Mongolia's Genghis Khan, whose horseback-riding warriors carved out a vast Eurasian empire. However, they galloped from a country with a miniscule GNP of its own—thus demonstrating that at the time military prowess was not handicapped by economic weakness.

2: The Rise of Asia and the Dispersal of Global Power

The rise to global preeminence of three Asian powers—Japan, China, and India—has not only altered dramatically the global ranking of power but also highlighted the dispersal of geopolitical power. The emergence of these Asian states as significant political-economic players is a specifically post–World War II phenomenon because none of them could exploit their population advantage until the second half of the twentieth century. Admittedly, inklings of Asia's emergence on the international scene first came into view with the brief rise of Japan as a major military power following its victory in the Russo-Japanese War of 1905. That unexpected triumph, however, was followed not long after by Japan's embrace of militaristic imperialism that ended in total defeat at the hands of the United States in 1945 in a war that the Japanese had proclaimed was aimed to free Asia from Western domination. The subsequent national recovery of Japan from its massive destruction in World War II provided the first major preview of an Asia whose economic growth signaled growing international stature.

The combination of a stable pacifist democracy, a national acceptance of American military protection, and a popular determination to rebuild the country's devastated economy created a fertile climate for Japan's rapid economic growth. Based on high rates of savings, moderate wages, deliberate concentration on high technology, and the inflow of foreign capital through energetically promoted exports, Japan's GDP grew from $500 billion in 1975 to $5.2 trillion in 1995.[2] Before long, Japan's economic success was emulated—though in politically more authoritarian settings—by China, South Korea, Taiwan, the Association of Southeastern Asian Nations (ASEAN) countries, and Indonesia, as well as by the more democratic India.

The relatively complacent American public of the mid-twentieth century at first paid little attention to Japan's new role in the world economy. But during the 1980s and early 1990s, American public anxiety suddenly focused on Japan. Public opinion was stimulated not by Japan's geopolitical assertiveness—for it possessed a pacifist constitution and was a steadfast American ally—but rather by Japanese electronic and then automobile products' highly visible domination of the American domestic market. US paranoia was fanned further by alarmist mass media reports of Japanese buyouts of key American industrial assets (and some symbolic ones: e.g., Rockefeller Center in New York City).

Japan came to be seen as an economic powerhouse, a trading giant, and even a growing threat to America's industrial and financial global preeminence. Japan as the new "superstate" became the fearsome and widely cited slogan of overblown media coverage and demagogic congressional rhetoric. Academic theories of America's inevitable decline in the face of the "rising sun" gave intellectual credence to widespread populist anxiety that only receded after Japan's "lost decade" of anemic economic growth during the 1990s.

Though fears of global economic domination by the Japanese were unrealistic, Japan's post–World War II recovery awakened the West to Asia's potential to assume a major economic and political role. And subsequent economic successes in the region, notably South Korea's similar drive, beginning in the 1960s, to establish an export-driven economy, further emphasized this point. By 2010, the president of the once-impoverished South Korea could assert confidently that his country was ready to play a significant role in global economic decision making; symbolically, Seoul even hosted a G-20 summit in 2010. Concurrently, both Taiwan and Singapore also emerged as dynamic examples of economic success and social development, with considerably higher rates of growth during the second half of the twentieth century than those attained by the Western European economies during their post–World War II recovery.

But these were merely a prelude to the most dramatic change in the world's geopolitical and economic pecking order: China's meteoric rise, by the first decade of the twenty-first century, into the front ranks of the leading world powers. The roots of that emergence go back many decades, beginning with the quest for national renewal launched more than a century ago by nationalistic young Chinese intellectuals and culminating some decades later in the victory of Chinese Communists. Although Mao's economically and socially devastating Great Leap Forward and Cultural Revolution set back China's rise for some years, the unprecedented takeoff in China's social and economic modernization started in 1978 with Deng Xiaoping's bold adoption of market liberalization, which "opened" China to the outside world and set it on a trajectory of unprecedented national growth. Its rise signals both the end of the West's singular preeminence and the concomitant shift eastward of the global center of gravity.

China's domestic reorientation coincided with a dramatic geopolitical realignment, its separation from the Soviet Union. Their gradual estrangement and growing mutual hostility broke into the open during the 1960s. That provided the United States with a unique opportunity, first explored by President Richard Nixon in 1972 and then consummated by President Jimmy Carter in 1978, to engage China in a common front against Moscow. In the course of the subsequent mere three decades, China, no longer faced by a potential Soviet threat and thus free to focus its resources on domestic development, achieved a degree of infrastructural modernization comparable to what had transpired in the West over the course of the previous century. Though faced with lingering internal ethnic challenges posed by Tibet and Xinjiang, a significant domestic political disruption in 1989, and socially painful inequality in rural and urban development, China's results were spectacular. However, they also eventually fueled American populist and geopolitical anxiety. Slogans about China "owning" the United States echoed the earlier uproar over Japanese purchases of American industrial and real estate assets during the late 1980s. By 2010, in an overreaction reminiscent of the earlier case of Japan, many feared that China would soon supplant America as the world's leading superpower.

The ongoing shift eastward in the distribution of global power has also been prompted by the recent emergence on the world scene of postcolonial India, one of the world's two most populous countries and a state also entertaining global ambitions. Contemporary India is a complicated mixture of democratic self-governance, massive social injustice, economic dynamism, and widespread political corruption. As a result, its political emergence as a force in world affairs has lagged behind

China's. India was prominent in sharing leadership of the so-called nonaligned nations, a collection of neutral but politically wavering states, including Cuba and Yugoslavia, all allegedly opposed to the Cold War. Its brief military collision with China in 1962, which ended in India's defeat, was only partially redeemed by its military successes in the two wars with Pakistan of 1965 and 1971. By and large, the prevailing view of India until relatively recently has been one of a country with strong moralistic opinions about world affairs but without commensurate influence.

This perception began to change as a consequence of two significant developments: India's defiant testing of its own nuclear device in 1974 and of nuclear weapons in 1998, and its period of impressive economic growth beginning in the 1990s. India's liberalizing reforms—including the deregulation of international trade and investment and the support of privatization—are transforming what was an anemic and cumbersome quasi-socialist economy into a more dynamic economy based on services and high technology, thus putting India on an export-driven growth trajectory similar to that of Japan and China. By 2010, India, with a population beginning to exceed China's, was even viewed by some as a potential rival to China's emerging political preeminence in Asia, despite India's persisting internal liabilities (ranging from religious, linguistic, and ethnic diversity to low literacy, acute social disparities, rural unrest, and antiquated infrastructure).

India's political elite is motivated by an ambitious strategic vision focused on securing greater global influence and a conviction of its regional primacy. And the gradual improvement in US-Indian relations during the first decade of the twenty-first century has further enhanced India's global stature and gratified its ambitions. However, its simmering conflict with Pakistan, which includes a proxy contest with it for greater influence in Afghanistan, remains a serious diversion from its larger geopolitical aspirations. Therefore, the view—held by its foreign policy elite—that India is not only a rival to China but also already one of the world's superpowers lacks sober realism.

Nonetheless, the appearance on the world scene of China as the economic challenger to America, of India as a regional power, and of a wealthy Japan as America's Pacific Ocean ally have not only altered dramatically the global ranking of power but also highlighted its dispersal. That poses some serious risks. The Asian powers are not (and have not been) regionally allied as in the case of the Atlantic alliance during the Cold War. They are rivals, and thus in some respects potentially similar to the European Atlantic powers during their colonial and then continental European contests for geopolitical supremacy, which eventually culminated in the devastation of World War I and World War II. The new Asian rivalry could at some point threaten regional stability, a challenge heightened in its destructive potential by the massive populations of the Asian powers and the possession by several of them of nuclear weapons.

There is, admittedly, a basic difference between the old transoceanic imperial rivalry of the European powers and that of the current Asian powers. The key participants in the Asian rivalry do not compete for overseas empires, which for Europe escalated distant collisions into great power conflicts. Regional flare-ups among them are more likely to occur within the Asia-Pacific region itself. Nonetheless, even a regionally confined collision between any of the Asian states (for example, over islands, or maritime routes, or watershed issues) could send shockwaves throughout the global economy.

The more immediate risk of the ongoing dispersal of power is a potentially unstable global hierarchy. The United States is still preeminent but the legitimacy, effectiveness, and durability of its leadership is increasingly questioned worldwide because of the complexity of its internal and external challenges. Nevertheless, in every significant and tangible dimension of traditional power—military, technological, economic, and financial—America is still peerless. It has by far the largest single national economy, the greatest financial influence, the most advanced technology, a military budget larger than that of all other states combined, and armed forces both capable of rapid deployment abroad and actually deployed around the world. This reality may not endure for very long but it is still the current fact of international life.

The European Union could compete to be the world's number two power, but this would require a more robust political union, with a common foreign policy and a shared defense capability. But unfortunately for the West, the post–Cold War expansion of the European Economic Community into a larger European "Union" did not produce a real union but a misnomer; in fact, the designations should have been reversed. The earlier smaller "community" of Western Europe was politically more united than the subsequently larger "union" of almost all of Europe, with the latter defining its unity through a partially common currency but without a genuinely decisive central political authority or a common fiscal policy. Economically, the European Union is a leading global player; it has a population and external trade considerably larger than that of the United States. However, through its cultural, ideological, and economic connections to America and more concretely through NATO, Europe remains a junior geopolitical partner to the United States in the semiunified West. The EU could have combined global power with global systemic relevance but, since the final collapse of their empires, the European powers chose to leave the more costly task of maintaining global security to America in order to use their resources to create a life-style of socially assured security (from the cradle throughout early retirement) funded by escalating public debts unrelated to economic growth.

As a consequence, the EU as such is not a major independent power on the global scene, even though Great Britain, France, and Germany enjoy a residual global status. Both Great Britain and France have been entitled since 1945, together with America, Russia, and China, to the right of veto in the UN Security Council and—like them—they also possess nuclear weapons. However, Great Britain remains wary of European unity while France is unsure of its larger global purpose. Germany is the economic engine of Europe and matches China in its exporting prowess but remains reluctant to assume military responsibilities outside of Europe. Therefore, these European states can only truly exercise global influence as part of the larger Union, despite all of the EU's current collective weaknesses.

In contrast, China's remarkable economic momentum, its capacity for decisive political decisions motivated by clearheaded and self-centered national interest, its relative freedom from debilitating external commitments, and its steadily increasing military potential coupled with the worldwide expectation that soon it will challenge America's premier global status justify ranking China just below the United States in the current international hierarchy. Symptomatic of China's growing self-confidence is its state-controlled media's frequent allusions to the increasing worldwide perception of China as America's emerging rival in global preeminence—despite China's residual and still-unresolved internal difficulties: rural vs. urban inequality and the potential of popular resentment of absolute political authority.

A sequential ranking of other major powers beyond the top two would be imprecise at best. Any list, however, has to include Russia, Japan, and India, as well as the EU's informal leaders: Great Britain, Germany, and France. Russia ranks high geopolitically largely because of its rich stores of oil and gas and its continued status as a nuclear power second only to the United States, though that military asset is diluted by its domestic economic, political, and demographic handicaps, not to mention the fact that from both the east and west it faces economically much more powerful neighbors. Without nuclear weapons or the dependence of some European states on Russian oil and gas, Russia would otherwise not rank very high on the pyramid of global geopolitical power. Economically, it lags significantly behind Japan, and a strategic choice by Japan to pursue a more active international role could elevate it above Russia as a major global player. India, regionally assertive and globally ambitious, is the new entrant into the presumptive top list, but it remains hindered by the strategic antagonism with its two immediate neighbors, China and Pakistan, as well as by its various social and demographic weaknesses. Brazil and Indonesia have already laid claims to participation in global economic decision making within the G-20 and aspire to take regional leadership roles in Latin America and in Southeast Asia, respectively.

The foregoing composition of the current global elite thus represents, as already noted, a historic shift in the global distribution of power away from the West as well as the dispersal of that power among four different regions of the world. In a positive sense, with the self-serving domination of major portions of the world by European powers now a thing of the past, these new realities of power are more representative of the world's diversity. The days when an exclusive Western club—dominated by Great Britain, France, or the United States—could convene to share global power at the Congress of Vienna, at the Versailles Conference, or at the Bretton Woods meeting, are irrevocably gone. But—given the persistence of historically rooted antagonisms and regional rivalries among the currently more diversified and geographically widespread ten leading powers—this new state of affairs also highlights the increased difficulty of consensual global decision making at a time when humanity as a whole is increasingly confronting critical challenges, some potentially even to its very survival.

It is far from certain how enduring that new convent of leading states will prove to be. One should be mindful of the fact that in the course of only one century—from approximately 1910 to 2010—the ranking hierarchy of global power changed significantly no less than five times, with all but the fourth signaling a divisive deterioration in the global preeminence of the West. First, on the eve of World War I the British and French empires were globally dominant and were allied to a weakened Tsarist Russia recently defeated by a rising Japan. They were being challenged from within Europe by the ambitious imperial Germany supported by a weak Austro-Hungarian and declining Ottoman empires. An industrially dynamic America, though initially neutral, made in the end a decisive contribution to the Anglo-French

FIGURE I.1 DECLINING IMPERIAL LONGEVITY

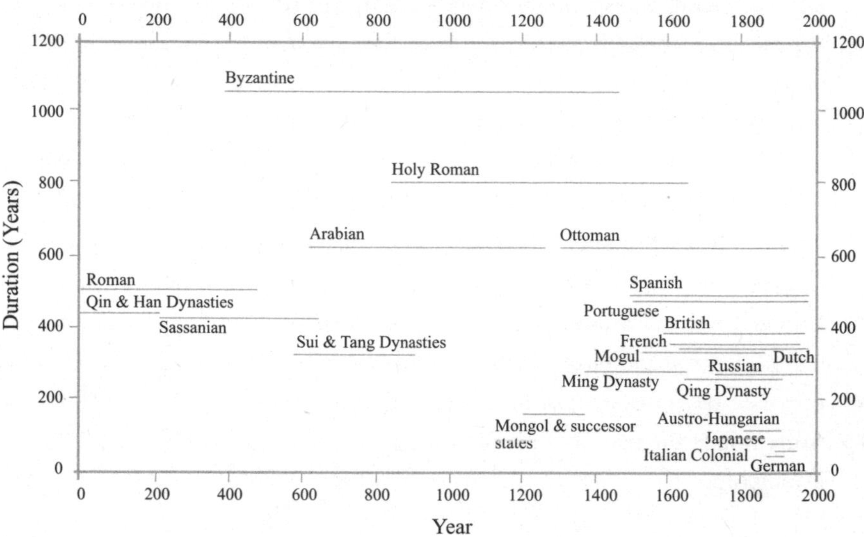

victory. Second, during the interlude between World War I and World War II, Great Britain seemed internationally preeminent, though with America clearly on the rise. However, by the early 1930s the rapidly rearming and increasingly revisionist Nazi Germany and Soviet Russia were already plotting against the status quo. Third, Europe was shattered by World War II, which produced in its wake the forty-year-long Cold War between the American and Soviet superpowers, the might of each overshadowing everyone else. Fourth, the ultimate "defeat" of the Soviet Union in the Cold War led to a brief unipolar phase in world affairs dominated by America as the sole global superpower. And, fifth, by 2010, with America still preeminent, a new and more complex constellation of power containing a growing Asian component was visibly emerging.

The high frequency of these power shifts signals a historical acceleration in the changing distribution of global power. Prior to the twentieth century, global preeminence by a leading state generally lasted for a century or so. But as conscious political activism became an increasingly widespread social phenomenon, politics became more volatile and global preeminence less enduring. The fact that the West remained globally dominant during the entire twentieth century should not obscure the fact that conflicts within the West undermined its once-dominant position.

Indeed, even today the uncertainty regarding the durability of America's current international leadership, the end of Europe's central role in world affairs as well as the EU's political impotence, Russia's nostalgia for a leading global role that it is incapable of exerting, the speculation that China before long might be ascending to global primacy, India's impatient ambition to be seen as a world power and its external as well as internal vulnerabilities, and Japan's lingering reluctance to translate its global economic weight into political assertiveness collectively reflect the reality of a more broadly based but less cohesive global leadership.

3: The Impact of Global Political Awakening

The ongoing dispersal of global power is furthered by the emergence of a volatile phenomenon: the worldwide political awakening of populations until recently politically passive or repressed. Occurring recently in Central and Eastern Europe and lately in the Arab world, this awakening is the cumulative product of an interactive and interdependent world connected by instant visual communications and of the demographic youth bulge in the less advanced societies composed of the easy-to-mobilize and politically restless university students and the socially deprived unemployed. Both groups resent the richer portions of humanity and the privileged corruption of their rulers. That resentment of authority and privilege is unleashing populist passions with unprecedented potential for generating large-scale turmoil.

The universal scope and the dynamic impact of this new social phenomenon is historically novel. For most of history, humanity has lived not only in compartmentalized isolation but also in a state of political stupor. Most people in most places were neither politically conscious nor politically active. Their daily lives were focused on personal survival in conditions of physical and material deprivation. Religion offered some solace while social traditions provided some degree of cultural stability and occasional collective relief from the hardships of fate. Political authority was remote, often seen as an extension of divine will, and frequently legitimated by hereditary entitlement. Struggles for power at the top tended to be confined to a narrow circle of participants, while group conflicts with adjoining communities focused largely on territorial or material possessions and were fueled by instinctive ethnic hatreds and/or divergent religious beliefs. Political conversations, political convictions, and political aspirations were a preoccupation of a privileged social stratum in the immediate vicinity of the ruler itself.

As societies became more complex, a distinctive class of people engaging in political discourse and in struggles for political power emerged at the apex of organized society. Whether in the court of the Roman or of the Chinese emperor, the courtiers or mandarins were active crypto-politicians, though focused more on palace intrigues than on wider policy issues. And as societies evolved even further and literacy increased, more participants entered the political dialogue: the landed aristocracy in the rural areas, wealthy merchants and artisans in the expanding towns and cities, and a limited elite class of intellectuals. Still, the populace at large remained politically disengaged and dormant, except for periodic outbreaks of violent but largely anarchistic outrage, as in the case of peasant uprisings.

The first socially inclusive but geographically limited manifestation of political awakening was the French Revolution. Its eruption was driven by a combination of atavistic rebellion from below and novel mass propagation from above. It occurred in a society in which a traditional monarchy was sustained by a politically literate but internally divided aristocracy and by a materially privileged Catholic Church. That power structure was then challenged by a politically literate but restless bourgeoisie engaged in public agitation in key urban centers and even by a peasantry increasingly aware of its relative deprivation.

Historically unprecedented political pamphleteering, facilitated by the printing press, rapidly translated social resentments into revolutionary political aspirations crystallized in emotionally captivating slogans: "*liberté, égalité, fraternité.*"

The resulting violent political upheaval produced a sudden unifying surge in collective and self-conscious national identity. Napoleon's military triumphs in the aftermath of the Revolution of 1789 owed at least as much to the collective fervor of a politically awakened French national identity as to his military genius. And that fervor spread rapidly throughout Europe, with its contagion first favoring Napoleonic victories and then contributing, in a rebound (having aroused Prussian, Austrian, and Russian nationalistic passions), to Napoleon's defeat. But by the "Spring of Nations" in 1848, much of Europe—notably Germany but also Italy, Poland, and soon Hungary—plunged into an age of fervent nationalism and socially self-conscious political awakening. By then, the more politically conscious Europeans had also become captivated by the democratic ideals of the socially less revolutionary but politically more inspirational humanism of the distant, open, and postaristocratic American republic.

However, less than a century later, Europe fell victim to wars inspired by its own conflicting populist passions. The two world wars coupled with the explicit anti-imperialism of the Bolshevik Revolution, helped make mass political awakening a global phenomenon. The conscripted soldiers of the British and French colonial empires returned home imbued with a new awareness of their own political, racial, and religious identity and of their economic privation. Concurrently, the increasing access to Western higher education and the resulting spread of Western ideas drew the minds of those in the upper strata of the indigenous populations of European colonies to captivating notions of nationalism and socialism.

Nehru of India, Jinnah of Pakistan, Sukarno of Indonesia, Nkrumah of Ghana, and Senghor of Senegal traveled such paths from their own personal political awakening to charismatic leadership in mass political

One of the most memorable moments in my public career occurred in 1978, when I was in Beijing to initiate secret efforts to normalize US-Chinese relations and to forge a de facto coalition of convenience against the then-expanding Soviet Union. Following the very sensitive and narrowly held negotiations with Deng, I was unexpectedly invited by him to a private dinner. As we sat in a pavilion overlooking a small lake within the Forbidden City and I quizzed him about the evolution of his own political views, he began to reminisce about his youth. Our talk turned to his expedition, as a very young student, from central China (first by a riverboat to the coast, and then by a steamer) to the then-so-remote Paris of the 1920s. It was for him at the time a trip literally into the distant unknown. He told me how gripped he became by the awareness of China's relative social retardation compared to France and how his sense of national humiliation made him turn for historical guidance to Marxist teachings about social revolution as a shortcut to national redemption. That was when his national resentment, political awakening, and ideological formation fused into one, and came to shape his subsequent participation in two revolutions: under Mao, to break with China's past, and then (when he became the leader) to shape China's future. Less than a year after that memorable moment, Deng Xiaoping and his wife—in the course of the Chinese leader's state visit to America—in a unique gesture, came to a private dinner at my home in the Washington suburbs.

proselytization, culminating in their leadership of respective national emancipations. Japan's sudden burst into world politics at the turn of the twentieth century also stimulated a parallel political awakening in China, then smarting under the humiliating subordination imposed on it by the European powers. Sun Yat-sen launched his quest for China's renewal in the early twentieth century having benefited from personal observation of Japan's self-initiated Western-style modernization; while another young Chinese, Deng Xiaoping, absorbed Marxism as a young student in distant Paris.

Over the course of two centuries, the revolution in mass communication and the gradual spread of literacy, especially among the growing concentration of urban residents, transformed individual political awakening into a mass phenomenon. Pamphleteering and the emergence of regularly published newspapers during the nineteenth century began to stoke popular desires for political change. As people in the middle and upper classes took on the habit of regularly reading newspapers, their political awareness grew and political dialogue about the state of national affairs became a normal social occurrence. The appearance of radio in the early twentieth century then gave political oratory a nationwide reach (think of Hitler) while giving even distant events a sense of dramatic immediacy, exposing hitherto politically passive and semi-isolated peoples to a cacophony of political clamor.

The recent emergence of global television, and then of the Internet, has in turn connected previously isolated populations with the world at large, and also augmented the ability of political activists to reach out to and mobilize the political loyalty and emotions of millions. The universal connectivity of the late twentieth century transformed political unrest into a worldwide learning process of street tactics in which otherwise disparate and distant political factions can borrow tactics from one another. Slogans quickly spread from Nepal to Bolivia, as have colored scarves from Iran to Thailand, videos of suffering from Sarajevo to Gaza, and tactics of urban demonstrations from Tunis to Cairo—all promptly ending up on TV and computer screens throughout the world. Thanks to these new means of communication, mass political agitation now involves a rapid geographical leapfrogging of shared experience.

In some countries, demographic "youth bulges"—disproportionately large populations of young adults who confront difficulties in their cultural and economic assimilation—are especially explosive when combined with the revolution in communication technology. Often educated but unemployed, their resulting frustration and alienation make them ideal recruits for militant groups. According to a 2007 report by Population Action International, youth bulges were present in a full 80% of civil conflicts between 1970 and 1999. It is also noteworthy that the Middle East and the broader Muslim world have a higher than average proportion of youth. Iraq, Afghanistan, the Palestinian territories, Saudi Arabia, and Pakistan all have massive youth populations whom their economies are unable to absorb and who are susceptible to disaffection and militancy. It is in this region, from east of Egypt to west of China, that accelerating political awakening has the greatest potential for violent upheaval. It is in effect a demographic powder keg. Similarly dangerous demographic realities prevail in African countries such as the Congo and Nigeria as well as in some Latin American countries.

The younger generation of today is particularly responsive to political awakening because the Internet and cellular phones liberate these young adults from their often-confining local political reality. They are also the political mass most inclined to militancy. In much of today's world, the millions of university students are thus the equivalent of Marx's concept of the "proletariat": the restless, resentful postpeasant workers of the early industrial age, susceptible to ideological agitation and revolutionary mobilization. Political sloganeering through the mass media can translate their often-inchoate sentiments into simple and focused formulations and action prescriptions. The more the latter can be related to specific resentments and deeply felt emotions, the more politically mobilizing they become. Not surprisingly, discourses about democracy, rule of law, or religious tolerance resonate less. In some cases, Manichean visions—rooted in reactions to subjectively felt racial, ethnic, or religious humiliations—have a more powerful appeal, such as in Iran in 1979. They explain better what the young feel while legitimating their thirst for retribution and even revenge.

The popular uprisings in North Africa and the Middle East during the first few months of 2011 provide a particularly vivid example of the potential consequences of the accelerating political awakening, characterized by the convergence of disaffected youth bulges with increasingly accessible mass communication technology. They were driven by resentment against corrupt and unresponsive national leaderships. Local frustrations with unemployment, political disfranchisement, and prolonged periods of "emergency" laws provided the immediate motivating impulse. Leaders who had been secure in their rule for decades found themselves suddenly confronted by the political awakening that had been gestating in the Middle East since the end of the imperial era. The interaction between the disenfranchised but politically aroused youth populations of the Middle East and the revolution in communication technology is now an important reality of geopolitics in this century.

In its very early phases, political awakening tends to be most impatient and prone to violence. Its passion is fueled by a deep sense of historically aggrieved self-righteousness. In addition, early political awakening is characterized by a focus on national, ethnic, and religious identity—especially identity defined by opposition to a detested external force rather than by abstract political concepts. Thus, populist nationalisms in Europe were initially ignited by opposition to Napoleon's conquests. Japanese political stirrings in the late Tokugawa period of the nineteenth century first took the form of antiforeign agitation and then turned by the first half of the twentieth century into an expansionist and militaristic nationalism. Chinese opposition to imperial domination surfaced violently in the Boxer Rebellion at the turn of the twentieth century and gradually led to a nationalistic revolution and civil wars.

In today's postcolonial world, the newly politically awakened partake of a common historical narrative that interprets their relative deprivation, prolonged external domination, denial of self-dignity, and continued personal disadvantage as the collective legacy of Western domination. Its anticolonial sharp edge is aimed at the West, fed by still vivid memories of British, French, Portuguese, Spanish, Belgian, Dutch, Italian, and German colonialism. In Muslim countries of the Middle East, even despite the fascination of many young Muslims with American mass culture, the intense resentment against American military intrusion in the Middle East as well as its support of Israel is now seen also as an extension of Western imperialism and thus as a major source of their felt deprivation.*

A prescient analysis of this phenomenon concluded, shortly after the end of the Cold War, that "one common and fundamental ingredient in cultural non-Westernisms today is a profound resentment against the West,"[3] citing as an evocative example the poem "Vultures" by the Senegalese poet, David Diop:

In those days,
When civilization kicked us in the face
When holy water slapped our cringing brows
The vultures built in the shadow of their talons
The blood stained monument of tutelage . . .

The poem encapsulated the anti-imperialist sentiment of a significant part of the new intelligentsia in the postcolonial regions. If such hostile views of the West were to become the universal mindset of the politically activated populations of the emerging countries, the more benign democratic values that the West was so hopefully propagating at the outset of the twenty-first century could become historically irrelevant.

---

* In a Pew 2010 survey, the percentage of respondents who held a favorable view of the United States was 17% in Turkey, 17% in Egypt, 21% in Jordan, 52% in Lebanon, and 17% in Pakistan. In that same survey, the percentage of respondents who believed that the United States considers their country's interests when making foreign policy either a "great deal" or "a fair amount" was 9% in Turkey, 15% in Egypt, 26% in Jordan, 19% in Lebanon, and 22% in Pakistan.

In a Pew 2008 survey, the percentage of respondents who associated selfishness with people in Western countries was 81% in Indonesia, 73% in Jordan, 69% in Turkey, 67% among British Muslims, 63% in Egypt, 57% among German Muslims, 56% in Nigeria, 54% in Pakistan, 51% among French Muslims, and 50% among Spanish Muslims. In that same survey, the percentage of respondents who associated arrogance with people in Western countries was 74% in Nigeria, 72% in Indonesia, 67% in Turkey, 64% among British Muslims, 53% in Pakistan, 49% in Egypt, 48% in Jordan, 48% among German Muslims, 45% among French Muslims, and 43% among Spanish Muslims.

Two further and indirect consequences of the phenomenon of global political awakening are also noteworthy. The first is that it marks the end of relatively inexpensive and one-sided military campaigns by technologically superior expeditionary forces of the West against politically passive, poorly armed, and rarely united native populations. During the nineteenth century native fighters in head-on battles against the British in Central Africa, against the Russians in the Caucasus, or against the Americans by Indians typically suffered casualties at a ratio of 100:1 in comparison to their well-organized and much better armed opponents. In contrast, the dawn of political awakening has stimulated a wider sense of shared commitment, greatly increasing the costs of external domination, as demonstrated in recent years by the highly motivated, much more persistent, and tactically unconventional popular resistance ("the people's war") of the Vietnamese, Algerians, Chechens, and Afghans against foreign domination. In the resulting battles of will and of endurance, the technologically more advanced were not necessarily the winners.

Second, the pervasive spread of political awakening has given special importance to a previously absent dimension of competitive world politics: global systemic rivalry. Prior to the onset of the industrial age, military prowess (weaponry, organization, motivation, training, and strategic leadership), backed by an adequate treasury, was the central and determining asset in the quest for a dominant status, with the issue often resolved by just one decisive land or sea battle.

In our time, comparative societal performance, as popularly judged, has become a significant component of national influence. Before 1800, no attention was paid to comparative social statistics—nor were they readily available—in the rivalries of France vs. Great Britain, or Austria-Hungary vs. the Ottoman Empire, not to mention China vs. Japan. But in the course of less than a century, societal comparisons have become increasingly important in shaping competitive international standings in public approval, especially for the top protagonists such as the United States and the USSR during the Cold War, or currently the United

States and China. Discriminating awareness of varying social conditions is now commonplace. Rapid and extensive access to international news and information, availability of numerous social and economic indexes, growing interactions between geographically distant economies and stock exchanges, and widespread reliance on television and the Internet all produce a continuous flow of comparative assessments of the actual performance and future promise of all major social systems. The systemic rivalry among major contenders is now scrutinized continuously, and its future outcome is currently seen by the world at large as especially dependent on the relative performance—carefully measured and projected even decades ahead—of the economies and social systems of America and China respectively.

The broad effect is a world that is now shaped to an unprecedented degree by the interaction of popular emotions, collective perceptions, and conflicting narratives of a humanity no longer subjectively submissive to the objective power of one politically and culturally specific region. As a result, the West as such is not finished, but its global supremacy is over. That, in turn, underlines the central dependence of the West's future role on America, on its domestic vitality, and on the historical relevance of its foreign policy. How the American system performs at home, and how America conducts itself abroad will determine the place and role of the West in the new objective and subjective global context. Both issues are wide open today, and ultimately their constructive resolution is America's current and unique historical responsibility.

The continued attraction of the American system—the vital relevance of its founding principles, the dynamism of its economic model, the good will of its people and government—is therefore essential if America is to continue playing a constructive global role. Only by demonstrating the capacity for a superior performance of its societal system can America restore its historical momentum, especially in the face of a China that is increasingly attractive to the third world. For example, when the United States presented itself as the undisputed champion of anticolonialism at the end of World War II, America became the preferred alternative—primarily in contrast to Great Britain—for those states seeking to bring themselves into modernity via free enterprise. A state perceived by others to be riding the crest of history finds it less difficult to secure its interests. And, while there is yet no explicitly ideological alternative to the United States in this new century, China's continued success could become a systemic alternative if the American system became widely viewed as an irrelevant model.

In such a case, the West as a whole could be in jeopardy. America's historic decline would undermine the political self-confidence and international influence of Europe, which then would be standing alone in a potentially more turbulent world. The European Union—with its aging population, lower rates of growth, even larger public debts than America's, and, at this stage of its history, the lack of a shared "European" ambition to act as a major power—is unlikely to be able to replace America's once-compelling attraction or fill its global role.

The EU thus faces potential irrelevance as a model for other regions. Too rich to be relevant to the world's poor, it attracts immigration but cannot encourage imitation. Too passive regarding international security, it lacks the influence needed to discourage America from pursuing policies that have intensified global cleavages, especially with the world of Islam. Too self-satisfied, it acts as if its central political goal is to become the world's most comfortable retirement home. Too set in its ways, it fears multicultural diversity. With one half of the geopolitical West thus disengaged from active participation in ensuring global geopolitical stability at a time when the world's new pecking order of power lacks coherence and a shared vision of the future, global turmoil and a rise in political extremism could become the West's unintended legacy.

Paradoxically, that makes the self-revitalization of America more crucial than ever.

- PART 2 -

The Waning of the American Dream

AMERICA, FOR BETTER OR FOR WORSE, IS THE FOCUS OF GLOBAL attention. More than any other country, America's multiethnic democracy has been and is the object of fascination, envy, and even occasional hostility on the part of the politically conscious global masses. That fundamental reality gives rise to some critical questions: Is the American system still an example worthy of worldwide emulation? Do the politically awakened masses see America as the hopeful portent of their own future? Do they view America as a positive influence in world affairs? Given that America's capacity to influence international events constructively depends on how the world perceives its social system and its global role, it follows that America's standing in the world will inevitably decline if negative domestic realities and internationally resented foreign initiatives delegitimize America's historical role. Therefore, the United States, with all its inherent and historically unique strengths, must overcome its staggering domestic challenges and reorient its drifting foreign policy in order to recapture the admiration of the world and revive its systemic primacy.

1: The Shared American Dream

Over the decades, the "American dream" has captivated millions and drawn them to America's shores. It is not an accident that America continues to attract the most motivated, not only among the already highly educated or those seeking a higher education but also among those determined to break out of the enslaving cycle of poverty in their own less-privileged societies. Many foreign scientists, doctors, and entrepreneurs still see more rewarding professional opportunities for themselves in America than at home. Their younger counterparts seek access to American graduate schools because an advanced degree from the United States enhances their career opportunities both at home and abroad. Many of the almost 1 million students who study here each year remain, seduced by America's opportunities. Similarly, the impoverished Central Americans who in some cases risk their lives to gain access to America's low-skill job market make an individual choice that sets them apart from those who do not dare embark on such a risky journey. For such motivated individuals, America still stands out as the world's most attractive shortcut to a much-improved life. And America has been the ultimate beneficiary of their driving personal dreams.

The key to America's prolonged historical appeal has been its combination of idealism and materialism, both of which are powerful sources of motivation for the human psyche. Idealism expresses the best in human instincts for it sanctifies the prioritizing of others over oneself and requires social and political respect for the intrinsic sacredness of all humans. The framers of America's Constitution encapsulated that idealism by seeking to structure a political system that protected shared fundamental assumptions regarding the "inalienable rights" of the human being (though shamefully not outlawing slavery). Political idealism became thus institutionalized. At the same time, the very reality of America's open spaces and absence of a feudal tradition made the material opportunities of the newly emergent country, with its unlimited frontiers, appealing to those who desired not only personal emancipation but also self-enrichment. On both scores, citizenship and entrepreneurship, America offered what Europe and the rest of the world then lacked.

The twin appeals of idealism and materialism defined America from the very start. It also attracted from across the Atlantic people who desired for their own homelands the promise inherent in the American Revolution. Whether it was Lafayette of France or Kosciuszko of Poland during the American war of independence, or Kossuth of Hungary in the mid-nineteenth century, their personal commitment to America popularized in Europe the image of a new type of society worthy of emulation. European admiration was further stirred by de Tocqueville's trenchant dissection of the workings of the new American democracy and by Mark Twain's captivating glimpses of the unfettered uniqueness of America's frontier life.

But none of that would have been as uniquely attractive to the immigrant masses flocking early on to America were it not for the young nation's abundant material opportunities. Free land and the absence of feudal masters beckoned. Economic expansion, fueled by the cheap labor of immigrants, created unprecedented business opportunities. Letters from immigrants to relatives back home spread a tempting vision, often a highly exaggerated one, of their personal success in the pursuit of the American dream. Alas, some would have to endure the painful discovery that America's streets were not in fact "paved with gold."

The absence of evident major external threats and the sense of secure remoteness (in contrast to the prevailing realities across the ocean), the new awareness of personal and religious freedom, and the temptation of material opportunities on the open frontier made the idealization of this new way of life synonymous with the reality. It also helped to obscure, and even justify, what otherwise should have been profoundly troubling: the progressive eviction and then extinction of the Indians (with the Indian Removal Act, passed by Congress in 1830, representing the first formalized case of ethnic cleansing), and the persistence of slavery followed by prolonged social repression and segregation of black Americans. But the broadly idealized version of American reality propagated by Americans themselves was not only a gratifying self-image; it was also widely shared abroad, especially in Europe.

As a consequence, a less-varnished image of the United States, entertained by America's immediate neighbor to the south, was largely ignored until some decades into the twentieth century. For Mexico, the new America was something very different: an expansionist and territorially greedy power, ruthless in its pursuit of material interests, imperialist in its international ambitions, and hypocritical in its democratic affectations. And while Mexican history itself is not above reproach, much of its national grievance against America was grounded in historical fact. America expanded at Mexico's expense, with an imperial momentum and territorial avarice not quite in keeping with the young American republic's attractive international image. Soon thereafter, the momentum of that expansion resulted in the planting of the American flag in the Hawaiian kingdom and some decades later even across the Pacific, in the Philippines (from which the United States withdrew only after World War II). Cuba and parts of Central America also had encounters with US power that were reminiscent of Mexico's experience.

Elsewhere, nineteenth- and early twentieth-century attitudes toward America were more mixed. Parts of South America were initially captivated by America's rejection of European domination, and some also imitated America's constitutional innovation. But the Monroe Doctrine, which barred European intervention in the Western Hemisphere, was viewed ambivalently, with some South American suspicions that its real motivation was self-serving. Political and cultural antagonism gradually surfaced, especially among the politically active parts of the middle-class intelligentsia. Two South American countries with regional ambitions, Peron's Argentina and Vargas' Brazil, explicitly challenged American regional domination during the twentieth century. The countries of Asia, geographically more remote and with their own political awakening delayed, were also vaguely attracted by America's remarkable material development but they lacked Europe's intellectual excitement and ideological affinity.

During the twentieth century, America's global standing twice reached soaring heights. Its first occurrence was in the immediate aftermath of World War I, and its second was at the end of the Cold War. America's then new international status was symbolized by President Wilson's idealistic Fourteen Points, which contrasted sharply with Europe's imperial and colonial legacies. To the practitioners of international power, it was evident that America's militarily significant intervention in World War I and, even more, its preeminent role in defining new principles of national self-determination for the intra-European rearrangements of power marked the entry on the world scene of a mighty state endowed with unique ideological and material appeal. That appeal was not diminished even by the fact that for the first time the idealized America was closing its gates to foreign immigration. More important, so it briefly seemed, was that America's new global engagement had began to reshape the basic patterns of international affairs.

However, the Great Depression a mere decade later was a warning signal of the American system's internal vulnerability and a jolt to America's global appeal. The sudden economic crisis, with its massive unemployment and social hardships, highlighted both the basic weaknesses and the iniquities of the American capitalist system as well as the related absence of an effective social safety net (with which Europe was just beginning to experiment). The myth of America as the land of opportunity persisted nonetheless, largely because the rise of Nazi Germany posed such a direct challenge to the values that Europe and America professed to share. Moreover, soon thereafter America became Europe's last hope once World War II broke out. The Atlantic Charter codified those shared but threatened values and acknowledged, in effect, that their survival was ultimately dependent on America's power. America also became the central point of refuge for European immigrants fleeing the rise of Nazism, evading the scourges of war, and increasingly fearing the spread of Communism. Unlike earlier times, a much higher percentage of the new arrivals were well educated, thus tangibly benefiting America's social development and international standing.

Shortly after the end of World War II, America faced a new challenge: that of systemic rivalry with the Soviet Union. The new rival was not only a serious competitor for global power, but it also offered an ambitious alternative of its own in response to humanity's quest for a better future. The combination of the Great Depression in the West and the emergence of the Soviet Union as World War II's major geopolitical victor—with Moscow by the late 1940s dominating much of Eurasia, including at the time even China—further enhanced the appeal of Soviet Communism. Its crude and more ideologically contrived combination of idealism and materialism thus contended on a global scale with the promise of the American dream.

From its revolutionary beginnings, the new Soviet state asserted that it was in the process of creating the world's first perfectly just society. Confident in the unique historical insights of Marxism, the USSR ushered in a new age of deliberately planned social innovation, allegedly based on egalitarian principles institutionalized coercively by an enlightened leadership. Coercive idealism in the service of rational materialism became the contagious utopian formula.

Though driven by mass terror, forced labor, large-scale deportations, and state-sponsored murder, the Soviet formula struck a chord with many in the politically awakened humanity shaken by two successive and enormously bloody wars. It was attractive to the poorer strata of the more advanced West, whose confidence in industrial progress was undermined by the Great Depression, to the increasingly anticolonial masses of Asia and Africa, and especially to radical intellectuals in search of historical certainty during a century of upheaval. Even shortly after the Bolshevik Revolution, when the experiment was barely under way in the midst of social deprivation and civil war, it drew affirmations of fealty from visiting foreign intellectuals reminiscent of America's early impact. "I have been over into the future, and it works," famously proclaimed a starry-eyed leftist American political writer, Lincoln Steffens, after a brief visit to Russia in 1919.

In the decades to follow, that conviction provided the framework for the widespread glorification of the Soviet experiment and for the indifference toward, and even the justification of, the unprecedented scale of its mass killings. Whether it was Jean-Paul Sartre or Kim Philby, Anglican clerics or Quaker preachers, anticolonial political activists from Asia or Africa, or even a former Vice President of the United States visiting a Soviet concentration camp that was presented to him as a social rehabilitation center, the notion that the Soviet Union's deliberately "rational" construction of the future was an improvement on America's largely spontaneous development became widely appealing in an age when for the first time social engineering seemed feasible.

The deceptive lure of the Soviet system was buttressed by claims that in the Soviet Union social equality, full employment, and universal access to medical care were actually becoming reality. In addition, by the mid-1960s, Soviet successes in the initial phase of the space competition with the United States, not to mention the buildup of Russia's nuclear arsenal, seemingly foreshadowed an inevitable Soviet triumph in the broader idealistic/materialistic rivalry with America. Indeed such an outcome was even officially predicted by Soviet leaders, who publicly asserted that by the 1980s the Soviet economy would outstrip America's.

This first overt systemic challenge to America came to an abrupt end a quarter of a century later, more or less at the time when the Kremlin expected the Soviet Union to achieve global systemic preeminence. For a variety of reasons—with some rooted in Soviet foreign policy errors and some in domestic ideological sterility, bureaucratic degeneration and socioeconomic stagnation, not to mention the mounting political unrest in Eastern Europe and hostility from China—the Soviet Union imploded. Its implosion revealed an ironic truth: Soviet claims to systemic superiority, so echoed by external admirers, were exposed as a sham in almost every social dimension. This grand failure had been obscured by the intellectually appealing pretense to "scientific" social management claimed by a ruling elite that cynically hid its privileges while exercising totalitarian control. Once that control cracked, the disintegrating Soviet political system unveiled a society of relative retardation and deprivation. In reality, the Soviet Union had been a rival to America in only one dimension: military power. And so, for the second time in the twentieth century, America stood peerless.

It seemed for a while after 1991 that America's triumph might last for a long time, with no rival in sight, imitation worldwide, and history seemingly halted. With systemic rivalry thus considered to be over, American leaders, in a somewhat ironic imitation of their fallen Soviet rivals, began to speak confidently of the twenty-first century as another American century. President Bill Clinton set the tone in his second inaugural address of January 20, 1997: "At this last presidential inauguration of the 20th century, let us lift our eyes toward the challenges that await us in the next century. . . . At the dawn of the 21st century . . . America stands alone as the world's indispensable nation." He was echoed, much more grandly, by his successor, President George W. Bush: "Our nation is chosen by God and commissioned by history to be a model for the world" (August 28, 2000).

But before long, the combination of China's impressive leap into the top ranks of the global hierarchy—resurrecting national anxiety dormant since Japan's spectacular economic rise during the 1980s—and America's growing indebtedness in the 2000s generated rising uncertainty regarding the longer-term durability of America's economic vitality. After 9/11, the vaguely defined "war on terror" and its expansion in 2003 into a unilateral war of choice against Iraq precipitated a widespread delegitimation of US foreign policy even among its friends. The financial crisis of 2008–2009 then shook global confidence in the United States' capacity to sustain its economic leadership over the long haul while simultaneously posing basic questions about the social justice and business ethics of the American system.

Yet even the financial crisis and the accompanying recession of 2007–2009—accompanied by shocking revelations of recklessly greedy speculation by Wall Street incompatible with basic notions of a socially responsible and productive capitalism—could not erase entirely the deeply ingrained image abroad of America's distinctive success in blending political idealism with economic materialism. It was striking how soon after that crisis the Chancellor of Germany, Angela Merkel, fervently proclaimed in a speech to the US Congress (November 3, 2009) her "passionate" commitment to "the American dream." She defined it as "the opportunity for everyone to be successful, to make it in life through their own personal effort," adding with great conviction that "there is still nothing that inspires me more, nothing that spurs me on more, nothing that fills me more with positive feelings than the power of freedom" inherent in the American system.

Merkel's message, however, carried with it an implicit warning of what it might mean for the West if the special image of the American way were to fade. And it did begin to fade, even before the crisis of 2008. America's image was most compelling at a time when it was viewed from a distance, as it was until the second half of the twentieth century, or when it was seen as the defender of the democratic West in two world wars, or as the necessary counterweight to Soviet totalitarianism, and especially so when it emerged as the clear victor of the Cold War.

But in the historically new setting of an America astride the world, America's domestic shortcomings were no longer shielded from close and critical scrutiny. Broad idealization of America gave way to more searching assessments. Thus, the world became more aware that America—despite being the hope of many who have the personal drive and ambition to become part of the "American dream"—is beset by serious operational challenges: a massive and growing national debt, widening social inequality, a cornucopian culture that worships materialism, a financial system given to greedy speculation, and a polarized political system.

2: Beyond Self-Delusion

Americans must understand that our strength abroad will depend increasingly on our ability to confront problems at home. Deliberate national decisions regarding necessary systemic improvements are now the essential precondition to any reasonable assessment of America's global prospects. This calls for clear-headed awareness on the part of Americans regarding their country's defining vulnerabilities as well as its residual global strengths. A coolheaded appraisal is the necessary point of departure for the reforms that are essential if America is to retain its position of global leadership while protecting the fundamental values of its domestic order.

Six critical dimensions stand out as America's major, and increasingly threatening, liabilities:

First is America's mounting and eventually unsustainable national debt. According to the Congressional Budget Office's August 2010 "Budget and Economic Outlook," American public debt as a percentage of GDP stood at around 60%—a troubling number, but not one that puts the United States in league with the worst global offenders (Japan's national debt, for example, stands at around 115% of GDP according to OECD net debt figures, though most of it is owned by the Japanese themselves; Greece and Italy each are at about 100%). But structural budgetary deficits driven by the imminent retirement of the baby boomer generation portend a significant long-term challenge. According to an April 2010 Brookings Institution study projecting the US debt under varied assumptions, the Obama administration's existing budget would have the US national debt surpass the post–World War II high of 108.6% of GDP by 2025. Given that paying for this spending trajectory would require a substantial tax increase for which as of now there is no national will, the inescapable reality is that growing national indebtedness will increase US vulnerability to the machinations of major creditor nations such as China, threaten the status of the US dollar as the world's reserve currency, undermine America's role as the world's preeminent economic model and, in turn, its leadership in such organizations as the G-20, World Bank, and IMF, and limit its ability to improve itself domestically and, at some point even, to raise the capital required to fight necessary wars.

America's grim prospects have recently been pithily summed up by two experienced public policy advocates, R. C. Altman and R. N. Haass, in their 2010 *Foreign Affairs* article "American Profligacy and American Power," in these grim words: "The post 2020 fiscal outlook is downright apocalyptic. . . . The United States is fast approaching a historic turning point: either it will act to get its fiscal house in order, thereby restoring the prerequisites of its primacy in the world, or it will fail to do so and suffer both the domestic and international consequences." If America continues to put off instituting a serious reform plan that simultaneously reduces spending and increases revenue, the United States will likely face a fate similar to the previous fiscally crippled great powers, whether ancient Rome or twentieth-century Great Britain.

Second, America's flawed financial system is a major liability. It presents twin vulnerabilities: First, it is a systemic time bomb that threatens not only the American but also the global economy because of its risky and self-aggrandizing behavior. And second, it has produced a moral hazard that causes outrage at home and undermines America's appeal abroad by intensifying America's social dilemmas. The excess, imbalance, and recklessness of America's investment banks and trading houses—abetted by congressional irresponsibility regarding deregulation and the financing of home ownership, and driven by greedy Wall

Street speculators—precipitated the financial crisis of 2008 and subsequent recession, inflicting economic hardship on millions.*

Making matters worse, financial speculators both in banks and in hedge funds, effectively immune to shareholder control, reaped enormous personal profits without the redeeming benefits of economic innovation or job creation. The 2008 crisis also revealed the striking disconnect already noted between the lives of those at the top of the financial system and the rest of the country, not to mention the developing world. In fact, according to a 2009 National Bureau of Economic Research working paper, the ratio of financial sector wages to those in the rest of the private economy exceeded 1.7 just prior to the 2008 financial crisis—levels not seen since before World War II. A reformation of the financial system through the implementation of simple but effective regulation, which increases transparency and accountability while promoting overall economic growth, is necessary to ensure that the United States remains economically competitive.

Third, widening income inequality coupled with stagnating social mobility is a long-term danger to social consensus and democratic stability,

---

* Roger Lowenstein's perceptive *The End of Wall Street* (New York: Penguin Press, 2010) contains the following telling data regarding the overall social and economic consequences of the self-induced 2008–2009 financial crisis:

Average deficits of G-20 nations increased from 1% to 8%. (294).

By 2009, each American share of the national debt was $24,000—$2,500 of which was debt to China (294).

America's total national wealth decreased from $64 trillion to $51 trillion (284).

America's unemployment rate reached 10.2%. (284).

The United States lost 8 million jobs (284).

Mortgage foreclosures increased from 74,000 a month in 2005 to 280,000 a month in the summer of 2008, and a high of 360,000 in July 2009 (147, 283).

Banks failed at a rate of three per week in 2009 (282).

During the spring of 2009, 15 million American families owed more on their mortgages than their homes were worth (282).

There was a total GDP contraction of 3.8%—the biggest contraction since post-WWII demobilization (282).

America experienced its longest recession since the 1930s (282).

Stocks fell 57%—the biggest drop since the Great Depression (281).

two conditions necessary for sustaining an effective US foreign policy. According to the US Census Bureau, since 1980 America has been experiencing a significant increase in income inequality: in 1980, the top 5% of households pocketed 16.5% of total national income, while the bottom 40% of households received 14.4%; by 2008, those disparities widened to 21.5% and 12%, respectively. The distribution not of annual income but of owned wealth by families was even more skewed: according to the Federal Reserve, in 2007 the richest 1% of US families possessed a staggering share of 33.8% of total net US national wealth, while the bottom 50% of American families accounted for only 2.5%.

This trend has launched the United States to the top of global indexes of both income and wealth inequality, making America the most unequal major developed country in the world (see Figures 2.1 and 2.2). Such income inequality might be more palatable if accompanied by social mobility, in keeping with notions of the American dream. But US social mobility has been essentially stagnant over the past few decades while at the same time income inequality has been rising. In fact, recent data for the Gini coefficient, a measure of income inequality cited in Figure 2.1, indicates that the United States ranks worst among the major economies, roughly on a par with China and Russia, with only Brazil among the major developing countries posting higher levels of inequality.

Moreover, recent studies comparing US intergenerational earnings mobility to those of various European countries show that overall economic mobility is actually lower in "the land of opportunity" than in the rest of the developed world. Worse still, America now lags behind some European countries in the rate of upward income mobility. One of the principal causes has been America's deficient public education system. According to the OECD, America spends one of the highest amounts per pupil on its primary and secondary education, yet has some of the lowest test scores in the industrialized world. That condition saps America's economic prospects by leaving swaths of human capital untapped while degrading the global appeal of the American system.

FIGURE 2.1 INCOME INEQUALITY
(From most unequal to least)

	YEAR	GINI COEFFICIENT
Brazil	2005	56.7
USA	2007	45.0
Russia	2009	42.2
China	2007	41.5
Japan	2008	37.6
Indonesia	2009	37.0
India	2004	36.8
UK	2005	34.0
France	2008	32.7
Italy	2006	32.0
EU	2009	30.4
Germany	2006	27.0

SOURCE: CIA World Factbook

FIGURE 2.2 SHARE OF TOTAL NATIONAL WEALTH

	YEAR, UNIT	TOP 10%	BOTTOM 50%	
USA	2001, family	69.8%	2.8%	
UK	2000, adult	56.0%	5.0%	
Japan	1999, household	39.3%	13.9%	
Italy	2000, household	48.5%	7.0%	(bottom 40%)
Indonesia	1997, household	65.4%	5.1%	
India	2002-03, household	52.9%	8.1%	
Germany	1998, household	44.4%	3.9%	
France	1994, person	61.0%	NA	
China	2002, person	41.4%	14.4%	
Canada	1999, family unit	53.0%	6.0%	
Australia	2002, household	45.0%	9.0%	

SOURCE: UN University, 2/2008 report

America's fourth liability is its decaying national infrastructure. While China is building new airports and highways, and Europe, Japan, and now China possess advanced high-speed rail, America's equivalents are sliding back into the twentieth century. China alone has bullet trains on almost 5,000 kilometers of rails, while the United States has none. Beijing and Shanghai airports are decades ahead in efficiency as well as elegance of their equivalents in Washington and in New York, both of which increasingly smack embarrassingly of the third world. On a symbolic level, the fact that China—in rural and small-town respects still a premodern society—is now moving ahead of the United States in such highly visible examples of twenty-first-century structural innovation speaks volumes.

The American Society of Civil Engineers, in its 2009 report card of America's infrastructure, put America's overall grade at an abysmal D; this included a D in aviation, a C– in rail, a D– in roads, and a D+ in energy. Urban renewal has been slow, with slums and deteriorating public housing in numerous cities—including even the nation's capital—a testimonial to social neglect. A mere train ride from New York City to Washington, DC (on the slow-moving and shaking Acela, America's "high-speed" train) offers from its railcar windows a depressing spectacle of America's infrastructural stagnation, in contrast to the societal innovation that characterized America during much of the twentieth century.

Reliable infrastructure is essential to economic efficiency and economic growth and simultaneously symbolic of a nation's overall dynamism. Historically, the systemic success of leading nations has been judged, in part, on the condition and ingenuity of national infrastructure—from the roads and aqueducts of the Romans to the railroads of the British. The state of American infrastructure, as indicated above, is now more representative of a deteriorating power than of the world's most innovative economy. And, as America's infrastructure continues to decay it will inevitably impact its economic output, probably at a time of even greater competition with emerging powers. In a world where systemic rivalry between the United States and China is likely to intensify, decaying infrastructure will be both symbolic and symptomatic of the American malaise.

America's fifth major vulnerability is a public that is highly ignorant about the world. The uncomfortable truth is that the United States' public has an alarmingly limited knowledge of basic global geography, current events, and even pivotal moments in world history—a reality certainly derived in part from its deficient public education system. A 2002 National Geographic survey found that a higher percentage of eighteen- to twenty-four-year-olds in Canada, France, Japan, Mexico, and Sweden could identify the United States on a map than their American counterparts. A 2006 survey of young American adults found that 63% could not point out Iraq on a map of the Middle East, 75% could not find Iran, and 88% could not locate Afghanistan—at a time of America's costly military involvement in the region. Regarding history, recent polls have shown that less than half of college seniors knew that NATO was formed to resist Soviet expansion and over 30% of American adults could not name two countries that America fought in World War II. Moreover, the United States lags behind other developed countries in these categories of public awareness. A 2002 National Geographic survey comparing current events and geography knowledge of young adults in Sweden, Germany, Italy, France, Japan, the UK, Canada, the United States, and Mexico found that the United States ranked second to last—barely beating out its less-developed neighbor, Mexico.

That level of ignorance is compounded by the absence of informative international reporting readily accessible to the public. With the exception of perhaps five major newspapers, local press and American TV provides very limited news coverage about world affairs, except for ad hoc coverage of sensational or catastrophic events. What passes for news tends to be trivia or human-interest stories. The cumulative effect of such widespread ignorance makes the public more susceptible to demagogically stimulated fear, especially when aroused by a terrorist attack. That, in turn, increases the probability of self-destructive foreign policy initiatives. In general, public ignorance creates an American political environment more hospitable to extremist simplifications—abetted by interested lobbies—than to nuanced views of the inherently more complex global realities of the post–Cold War era.

The sixth liability, related to the fifth, is America's increasingly gridlocked and highly partisan political system. Political compromise has become more elusive, in part because the media, especially TV, talk radio, and political blogs, are increasingly dominated by vitriolic partisan discourse while the relatively uninformed public is vulnerable to Manichean demagogy. As a result, political paralysis often precludes the adoption of needed remedies, as in the case of deficit reduction. This, in turn, fuels the global impression of American impotence in the face of pressing social needs. Furthermore, America's existing political system—highly dependent on financial contributions to political campaigns—is increasingly vulnerable to the power of well-endowed but narrowly motivated domestic and foreign lobbies that are able to exploit the existing political structure in order to advance their agendas at the expense of the national interest. Worst of all, according to a careful RAND Corporation study, "a process with roots as large and as deep as political polarization is unlikely to be reversed easily, if at all. . . . Our nation is in for an extended period of political warfare between the left and the right."[1]

The foregoing six conditions currently provide ammunition for those already convinced of America's inevitable decline. They also prompt negative comparisons with the cradle-to-the-grave paternalism of the relatively prosperous Europe. The European model—endowed in recent decades with higher international standing thanks to the combined financial-trading might of the European Union—has in recent years come to be seen by many as socially more just than the American model. However, on closer scrutiny, it has become more apparent that the European system writ large shares some of the above-mentioned negatives of its American counterpart, with potentially serious vulnerabilities for its long-term vitality. In particular, the Greek and later the Irish debt crises of 2010 and their contagion effects suggested that the paternalism and social generosity of the European economic system are potentially unsustainable and could eventually threaten Europe's financial solvency, a realization taken recently to heart by the conservative leadership in the UK, leading to austerity measures forcing dramatic cuts in social welfare programs.

At the same time, as mentioned earlier, it is a fact that Europe has higher rates of social equality and mobility than America, despite America's traditional reputation as "the land of opportunity." Its infrastructure, especially in environmentally prudent public transport such as high-speed rail, is superior to America's dilapidated airports, train stations, roads, and bridges. It also has a more geographically literate and internationally informed population that is less vulnerable to fear-mongering (despite the existence of fringe nationalist/racist parties on the right) and thus also to international manipulation.

Alternatively, China is often considered the wave of the future. However, given its social retardation and political authoritarianism, it is not America's competitor as a model for the relatively more prosperous, more modern, and more democratically governed states. But, if China continues on its current trajectory and averts a major economic or social disruption, it could become America's principal competitor in global political influence, and even eventually in economic and military might. The nonegalitarian and materialistically motivated dynamism of Chinese modernization already offers an appealing model to those parts of the world in which underdevelopment, demographics, ethnic tension, and in some cases negative colonial legacy have conspired to perpetuate social backwardness and poverty. For that portion of humanity, democracy vs. authoritarianism tends to be a secondary issue. Conceivably, a democratic and developing India could be China's more relevant rival—but in overcoming such key social liabilities as illiteracy, malnutrition, poverty, and infrastructural decay, India is not yet competitive with China.

AMERICA'S BALANCE SHEET

LIABILITIES	ASSETS
National Debt	Overall Economic Strength
Flawed Financial System	Innovative Potential
Widening Social Inequality	Demographic Dynamics
Decaying Infrastructure	Reactive Mobilization
Public Ignorance	Geographic Base
Gridlocked Politics	Democratic Appeal

3: America's Residual Strengths

The table above summarizing America's liabilities and assets points to a critical proposition regarding the American system's capacity to compete globally: the foreseeable future (i.e., the next two decades) is still largely America's to shape. The United States has the capacity to correct its evident shortcomings—if it takes full advantage of its considerable strengths in the following six key areas: overall economic strength, innovative potential, demographic dynamics, reactive mobilization, geographic base, and democratic appeal. The basic fact, which the currently fashionable deconstruction of the American system tends to slight, is that America's decline is not foreordained.

The first crucial asset is America's overall economic strength. America is still the world's largest national economy by a good margin. Only the economically united European region slightly surpasses the United States, but even so the Western European model exhibits higher structural unemployment and lower rates of growth. More significant for future trends is the fact that the United States, despite Asia's rapid economic growth, has maintained for several decades its major share of the world's GDP (see Figure 2.3). Its 2010 GDP of over $14 trillion accounted for just around 25% of global output, while its closest competitor, China, made up over 9% of global output with a close to $6 trillion

FIGURE 2.3 PERCENTAGE SHARE OF GLOBAL GDP

	1970	1980	1990	2000	2010
US	27.26	26.18	26.76	28.31	26.30
Europe	35.92*	33.77	31.70	31.92	28.30
China	0.78*	1.00	1.80	3.72	7.43
India	0.87	0.82	1.07	1.40	2.26
Russia	4.27*	4.09	3.84	1.50	1.86
Japan	9.84	10.68	11.88	10.25	8.74

SOURCE: Economic Research Service, USDA, International Macroeconomic Data Set (12/22/10 update)

*The figures for Europe for 2000 and 2010 include all 27 members of the EU, and the other Europe data pertains to the "EU15"; Russia is calculated as the former Soviet Union for 1970, 1980, and 1990, and the Russian Federation for 2000 and 2010; China's share of GDP is now greater than Japan's—ERS has not updated since China's economy over took Japan's in late 2010/early 2011.

GDP. The Carnegie Endowment for International Peace estimates that the United States will go from having a $1.48 trillion smaller GDP than the EU in 2010 to a $12.03 trillion larger GDP than the EU in 2050; and in terms of per capita GDP, the United States will increase its lead over the EU from $12,723 in 2010 to $32,266 in 2050.

It is true that according to current forecasts, China, largely due to its overwhelming population base, will surpass the United States in total economic size sometime in the twenty-first century; the Carnegie Endowment puts that date around 2030. For similar reasons, although not at the same speed, India should climb up the global GDP ranks over the next forty years as well. But neither China nor India will come even close to US levels in per capita GDP (see Figure 2.4). Thus, neither China, nor India, nor Europe can match the United States in its potent economic mix of overall size and high per capita GDP. This economic advantage—assuming America also exploits its other assets—can preserve America's global economic clout and systemic appeal, as well as its suction effect on global talent.

FIGURE 2.4 PROJECTED GDP AND GDP PER CAPITA

GDP (2005 $; NOT PPP)	US	EU	CHINA	JAPAN	RUSSIA	INDIA
1) GDP 2010 (2005 $ trillion)	$13.15	$14.63	$3.64	$4.54	$0.88	$1.13
2) GDP 2025 (2005 $ trillion)	$19.48	$19.10	$16.12	$5.56	$2.01	$3.80
3) GDP 2030 (2005 $ trillion)	$22.26	$20.34	$21.48	$5.79	$2.49	$5.33
4) GDP 2050 (2005 $ trillion)	$38.65	$26.62	$46.27	$6.22	$4.30	$15.38
5) GDP Per Capita 2010 (2005 $)	$42,372	$29,649	$2,699	$35,815	$6,328	$966
6) GDP Per Capita 2025 (2005 $)	$54,503	$38,320	$11,096	$47,163	$15,714	$2,722
7) GDP Per Capita 2030 (2005 $)	$59,592	$40,901	$14,696	$50,965	$20,039	$3,648
8) GDP Per Capita 2050 (2005 $)	$88,029	$55,763	$32,486	$66,361	$39,350	$9,287

SOURCE: Carnegie Endowment for International Peace's The World Order in 2050, February 2010

FIGURE 2.5 QUALITATIVE ASSESSMENT OF THE UNITED STATES AND THE EMERGING POWERS*

AVERAGE RANKING ACROSS ECONOMIC INDICATORS *Averaged global ranking from Entrepreneurship, Economic Competitiveness, and Trade Logistics Indexes*	
Country	***Averaged Rank Worldwide***
United States	7th
China	31st
India	50th
Brazil	51st
Russia	71st

AVERAGE RANKING ACROSS SOCIAL AND POLITICAL INDICATORS *Averaged global ranking from Corruption, Human Development, Education, and Freedom of the Press Indexes*	
Country	***Averaged Rank Worldwide***
United States	20th
Brazil	75th
Russia	110th
India	111th
China	112th

*These two tables represent the averaged rankings of the United States, China, Russia, India, and Brazil across several international indexes that measure economic, social, and political development worldwide. While the United States ranks strongly ahead of the other major aspirants to global primacy in both economic and sociopolitical indicators, the United States does not rank first in any of these indexes when compared against all other countries. These two tables reveal that while the competition for global power is growing, no other emerging power exhibits the combination of soft and hard power that has defined America's global preeminence.

Partially driving America's economic success is its second major asset: technological and innovative prowess derived from an entrepreneurial culture and superiority in institutions of higher education. The United States is ranked by the World Economic Forum as having the fourth most competitive economy in the world behind Switzerland, Sweden, and Singapore, and a Boston Consulting Group ranking of the world's most innovative economies placed the United States above every large economy with the exception of South Korea.

Moreover, comparative assessments of other "softer" aspects of social vitality suggest that the United States still ranks relatively high in some key qualitative categories used to measure systemic performance in other major countries (see Figure 2.5). It is worrisome that America is not at the top, but more important for the near-term future is the fact that the major aspirants to the global elite perform markedly worse in most categories. That reinforces the point developed later regarding the absence in the near future of any effective substitute for America with the capacity to wield both the soft and the hard dimensions of international power.

Highly important in this regard is America's dominance in higher learning: according to a Shanghai Jiao Tong University ranking of top global universities, eight out of the top ten universities in the world are American, as are seventeen out of the top twenty. These institutions not only provide America the means and technical know-how to maintain an economic—and even military—edge in pioneering the products and industries of the future. They also add to the domestic accumulation of human capital, as top researchers, engineers, and entrepreneurs around the world immigrate to the United States in order to reach their full educational and economic potential. This fact should remind Americans of how critical their higher educational dominance is to their country's domestic vitality, international prestige, and global influence.

The third advantage is America's relatively strong demographic base, especially when compared to those of Europe, Japan, and Russia. America's large population of 318 million is an inherent source of global clout. Moreover, the United States does not suffer from nearly the same level of population aging, or even population decline, projected elsewhere. According to the UN, by 2050 the United States will have a population of 403 million, 21.6% of it above the age of sixty-five. During that time period, the EU will go from a population of 497 to 493 million, with 28.7% over the age of sixty-five in 2050. The numbers for Japan are even more striking: it will go from a population of 127 million in 2010 to 101 million in 2050, and will have a public that is 37.8% over sixty-five by midcentury (see Figure 2.6).

One of the reasons for this felicitous discrepancy is America's ability to attract and assimilate immigrants—despite recent domestic unrest about this subject. America currently has a net migration rate of 4.25 per thousand population; Germany attracts 2.19, the UK 2.15, France 1.47, Russia 0.28, and China –0.34. This ability to attract and assimilate foreigners both shores up America's demographic base and augments its long-term economic outlook and international appeal. If America yields to anti-immigrant and xenophobic tendencies, it could jeopardize the beacon effect that has proved so beneficial to America's dynamism, prosperity, and prospects.

The fourth asset is America's capacity for reactive mobilization. The pattern of its democratic politics is for delayed reactions, followed by social mobilization in the face of a danger that prompts national unity in action. That happened in warfare, with "Remember Pearl Harbor" becoming a slogan that helped to mobilize a national effort to turn America into a war-making arsenal. The race to the moon, once it gripped public imagination, had the effect of spurring massive technological innovation. America's current dilemmas beg for a similar effort, and some of America's liabilities provide ready-made foci for social mobilization on behalf of socially constructive goals. An attack on America's frayed and antiquated infrastructure is one obvious target. A green America, in response to global warming, could be another. With effective presidential summoning of popular support, America's material assets as well as entrepreneurial talents could be harnessed to undertake the needed domestic renewal.

FIGURE 2.6 PROJECTED TOTAL POPULATION AND AGING

TOTAL POPULATION (MILLIONS)	US	EU	CHINA	JAPAN	RUSSIA	INDIA
1) Population 2010	317.64	497.53	1,354.15	127.00	140.37	1,166.08
2) Population 2025	358.74	506.22	1,453.14	120.79	132.35	1,431.27
3) Population 2030	369.98	505.62	1,462.47	117.42	128.86	1,484.60
4) Population 2050	403.93	493.86	1,417.05	101.66	116.10	1,613.80

SOURCES: UN projections, assuming medium fertility variant (EU is EU 27)

AGING—POPULATION 65+	US	EU	CHINA	JAPAN	RUSSIA	INDIA
1) % of Total Population 2010	13.0%	17.5%	8.2%	22.6%	12.9%	4.9%
2) % of Total Population 2025	18.1%	22.0%	13.4%	29.7%	17.7%	7.3%
3) % of Total Population 2030	19.8%	23.8%	15.9%	30.8%	19.4%	8.4%
4) % of Total Population 2050	21.6%	28.7%	23.3%	37.8%	23.4%	13.7%
5) Current Life Expectancy at Birth (years)	78.11	78.67	73.47	82.12	66.03	66.09

SOURCES: (1-4) UN projections, assuming medium fertility variant, EU is EU 27; (5) CIA World Factbook.

Fifth, unlike some major powers, America has the advantage of a uniquely secure, natural resource–rich, strategically favorable, and very large geographic base for a population that is nationally cohesive and not beset by any significant ethnic separatism. America also is not threatened by the territorial ambitions of any neighbor. Its northern neighbor is a friend, and—truth be said—socially a more successful version of a shared way of life. Canada in its great geographic depth also enhances America's security. America's landmass is rich in natural resources, ranging from minerals to agriculture and increasingly also to energy, still much of which—especially in Alaska—is untapped. America's location on the edge of the world's two most important oceans—the Atlantic and the Pacific—offers a security barrier while America's shores provide a springboard for maritime commerce and, if necessary, for transoceanic power projection. In brief, no other major country enjoys all of these advantages as a permanent condition as well as a beneficial opportunity.

America's sixth asset is its association with a set of values—human rights, individual liberty, political democracy, economic opportunity—that are generally endorsed by its population and that over the years have enhanced the country's global standing. America has long benefited from this ideological advantage, exploiting it in recent years to prevail successfully in the Cold War. Subsequently, however, some of that appeal has waned, largely because of widespread international disapproval of the 2003 invasion of Iraq and its associated excesses. The latter notwithstanding, the broad view of America as fundamentally a democracy still retains its residual appeal. For example, according to the 2010 Pew Global Attitudes Survey, in 2007 US favorability ratings were at a ten-year low, as nations like Indonesia held only a 29% favorable view of the United States and even allies like Germany held only a 30% favorable view. However, those numbers rebounded in 2010 with, for example, Indonesia holding a 59% favorable view and Germany holding a 63% favorable view.

Hence the invigoration of America's positive international identification with its democratic traditions is both possible and desirable.

Such values have been, and again could be, an asset to America, especially in comparison with the authoritarian regimes in China and Russia. The fact that these two countries are unable to boast of a universally appealing political ideology, though the former Soviet Union made a futile effort to do so during its systemic rivalry with the United States, is to America's long-term advantage. While much of the world may resent the United States for its unilateral foreign policy actions, there is also a concerned awareness among many that a rapid US decline and isolationist retreat would set back prospects for stable international spread both of global economic development and of democracy.

The above six basic assets thus provide a powerful springboard for the historic renewal that America so badly needs. But the more difficult part of that renewal of relevance remains the urgent need to redress its already noted and potentially very serious systemic vulnerabilities. Remedies for coping with each major risk or deficiency do exist, and they are already the subject of lively national debates. It is not some mysterious historical determinants, but rather the continuing dearth of political will and national consensus to tackle the challenges that threaten America's long-term prospects.

Americans now widely recognize the importance of critical domestic reforms, such as broad financial overhaul and long-term fiscal balancing, to America's future domestic prosperity and constructive international role. Effectively addressing the deficiencies of America's secondary educational system would also go a long way toward shoring up America's long-term economic outlook because its qualitative improvement would redress many of the shortcomings mentioned earlier (notably inequality, social immobility, and public ignorance). Balancing the budget, financial reform, and addressing iniquitous income inequality all will require uncomfortable social tradeoffs in incentives, taxes, and regulations. Only a sense of shared social sacrifice in the pursuit of national renewal will generate the necessary solidarity at all societal levels.

Ultimately, America's long-term success in self-renewal may require a fundamental change of focus in America's social culture: how Americans define their personal aspirations and the ethical content of their national "dream." Is the acquisition of material possessions way beyond the requirements of convenience, comfort, and self-gratification the ultimate definition of the good life? Could patiently and persistently pursued domestic reforms turn America into an example of an intelligent society in which a productive, energetic, and innovative economy serves as the basis for shaping a society that is culturally, intellectually, and spiritually more gratifying? Unfortunately, such a far-reaching reevaluation of the meaning of a good life might occur only after the American public has been shocked into a painful understanding that America itself will be in jeopardy if it continues on a course that leads from the pursuit of domestic cornucopia to a plunge into international bankruptcy.

The next several years should provide a partial insight into the future. If political gridlock and partisanship continue to paralyze public policy, if they preclude a socially fair sharing of the costs of national renewal, if they disregard the dangerous social tendency that magnify income disparities, if they ignore the fact that America's standing in the global pecking order may be in jeopardy, the anxious prognosis of America's decline could become its historical diagnosis. But that is not inevitable. It does not need to be the case, given the residual strengths of contemporary America and its demonstrated capacity for a nationally focused response to a challenge. That was the case after the Great Depression and during World War II, in the 1960s during the Cold War, and it can be so again.

4: America's Long Imperial War

If the crash of 2007 provided an imperative lesson regarding the need to undertake a major reassessment of some of America's basic systemic features, domestic values, and social policies, the date 9/11 similarly should encourage America to rethink seriously whether it has intelligently exploited the extraordinary opportunity of the peaceful yet geopolitically successful end of the Cold War.

It is now easy to forget how threatening the Cold War really was during its long four and a half decades. A hot war could have broken out suddenly at any moment with a decapitating strike that in minutes could have eliminated the US leadership, and in hours incinerated much of the United States and Soviet Union. The "Cold" War was stable only in the sense that its fragile mutual restraint depended on the rationality of a few fallible human beings.

Following the disintegration of the Soviet Union in 1991, the United States reigned supreme. Its political values and its socioeconomic system basked in global admiration and were the object of eager imitation. Its international position faced no challenges. The transatlantic relationship with Europe was no longer primarily based on a shared fear but instead on a common faith in a larger Atlantic community in which Europe was expected to move expeditiously toward its own more genuine political unity. In the Far East, Japan—America's closest Asian ally—gradually ascended to international eminence. Fears that the Japanese "superstate" would take over America's assets quietly waned. Relations with China had continued to improve following diplomatic recognition back in 1978 and China even became America's partner in opposing the Soviet Union in Afghanistan in 1980. America's attitude toward China thus had become more positive and, if anything, America was unreasonably complacent in its self-deceiving view that China's domestic backwardness would for long prevent it from becoming America's viable competitor.

America was thus widely seen as the world's economic engine, political example, social beacon, and unchallengeable paramount power. Exploiting that advantage, it led, almost simultaneously, a successful global coalition evicting Iraq from its recently seized Kuwait—and did so with Russian support, Chinese compliance, and Syrian participation, not to mention the cooperation of America's traditional allies. But America failed in the years that followed to seize the moment and address the conundrum of the Israeli-Palestinian conflict. Since the war in 1967, the Middle Eastern problem had come to be—so to speak—owned by the United States as a result of its preeminent position in the region. However, except for President Carter's significantly successful promotion of an Israeli-Egyptian peace accord, the United States played a largely passive role, even during its globally dominant status throughout the 1990s. After the assassination in 1995 of Israel's realistic Prime Minister Yitzhak Rabin by an Israeli opponent of the peace process, a belated but futile effort by the United States to revive Israeli-Palestinian negotiations was attempted—but rather passively—only in the last six months of the eight-year Clinton presidency.

Soon thereafter came September 11, 2001—the culmination of increasingly violent Al Qaeda attacks on American targets throughout the 1990s. This tragic event provoked three major US reactions. First, President George W. Bush committed the United States to a military undertaking in Afghanistan not only to crush Al Qaeda and to overthrow the Taliban regime that had sheltered it, but also to shape in Afghanistan a modern democracy. Then, in early 2002 he endorsed the military operation undertaken by Prime Minister Sharon (whom he described as "a man of peace") to crush the PLO in the Palestinian West Bank. Third, in early spring of 2003 he invaded Iraq because of unsubstantiated accusations of an Iraqi connection with Al Qaeda and of its alleged possession of "weapons of mass destruction." Cumulatively, these actions heightened public animus toward the United States in the Middle East, enhanced Iran's regional standing, and engaged America in two interminable wars.

By 2010, the Afghan and Iraqi wars were among the longest in America's history. The first of these, undertaken within weeks of the terrorists' attack on New York City, which had produced the largest number of civilian casualties ever inflicted by an enemy on American society, precipitated a publically endorsed military reaction designed to destroy the Al Qaeda network responsible for the attack, and to remove from power the Taliban regime in Afghanistan, which had provided safe haven to the perpetrators. The second of these long wars was the early 2003 US military invasion of Iraq, supported from abroad only by a politically pliant British Prime Minister and by Israel, but otherwise opposed or viewed with skepticism by most of America's other allies. It was publicly justified by the US President on the basis of dubious

DURATION OF MAJOR US WARS
*(As of March 2011, in number of months, * denotes an active war)*

Afghanistan*	112
Vietnam	102
Independence	100
Iraq*	96
Civil War	48
World War II	45
Korea	37
Britain (1812)	32
Philippine insurrection	30
Mexico	21
World War I	20
Spain	3
Iraq (1991)	2

charges of Iraqi possession of WMDs, which evaporated altogether within a few months, with no supporting evidence ever found in US-occupied Iraq. Since this war commanded President Bush's enthusiasm, the war in Afghanistan was relegated to almost seven years of relative neglect.

These two wars had one common trait: they were expeditionary military operations in hostile territories. In both cases, the Bush administration showed little regard for the complex cultural settings, deeply rooted ethnic rivalries generating conflicts within conflicts, dangerously unsettled regional neighborhoods (especially involving Pakistan and Iran), and the unresolved territorial disputes, all of which severely complicated US actions in Afghanistan and Iraq and ignited wider regional anti-American passions. Though America's interventions were reminiscent of nineteenth-century punitive imperial expeditions against primitive and usually disunited tribes, in the new age of mass political awakening, warfare against aroused populism has become, as the United

States has painfully discovered, more protracted and taxing. Last but by no means least, in the age of global transparency, a total victory, achieved ruthlessly by any means necessary has ceased to be a viable option; even the Russians, who did not hesitate to kill hundreds of thousands of Afghans and who drove several million of them into exile, did not go all out in seeking to prevail.

At the same time, however, both the Afghan and Iraqi conflicts—much like the West's expeditionary wars of the past—left the American homeland largely unaffected, except of course for soldiers and their families. Though both wars cost America billions of dollars and though their totals were higher than of all previous wars except for World War II, their cost as a percentage of America's GDP was low because of the enormous expansion of the US economy. Moreover, the Bush administration refrained from increasing taxes in order to pay for the wars, financing them instead by more politically expedient borrowing, including from abroad. From a social perspective, the fact that the fighting and dying was being done by volunteers—unlike in the earlier Vietnamese and Korean wars—also reduced the societal scope of personal pain.

Insofar as the actual conduct of these wars is concerned, the several-years-long neglect of the War in Afghanistan in favor of the Iraq War was compounded by the Bush administration's use of a deliberately sweeping definition of terrorism as a justification for prioritizing the campaign against Saddam Hussein, ignoring Iraq's ideological hostility toward Al Qaeda and Al Qaeda's reciprocal animus toward Saddam's regime. By implicitly collating the two under the sweeping rubric of "Islamic jihad," and by making the "war on terror" the justification for US military reactions, it became easier to mobilize American public outrage at 9/11 against not only the actual perpetrators but also against other Islamic entities. The "mushroom cloud," said by Condoleezza Rice (then National Security Advisor) to be threatening America, thus became a convenient symbol for mobilizing public opinion against a newly designated and very sweeping target. It served to drive public fears to a high pitch, placing at a disadvantage those who dared to express reservations regarding the factual accuracy of the White House's case for war against Iraq.

Demagogy fueled by fear can be a potent tool, effective in the short run but with significant long-term domestic and foreign costs. Its pernicious effects can be seen in some of the more notorious cases of abuse of Iraqi prisoners, including of some senior Iraqi officers. They were the byproducts of an atmosphere in which the enemy came to be seen as the personification of evil, and thus justifiably the object of personal cruelty. American mass media—including Hollywood movies and TV dramas—likewise contributed significantly to shaping a public mood in which fear and hatred were visually focused on actors with personally distinctive Arab features. Such demagogy inspired discriminatory acts against individual Muslim Americans, especially Arab Americans, ranging in scope from racial profiling to broad indictments against Arab American charities. Cumulatively, infusing into the "war on terror" a racial as well as religious dimension tarnished America's democratic credentials, while the decision to go to war against Iraq a year and a half after 9/11 became a costly diversion.

It could have been—and should have been—otherwise. First of all, the Iraq War was unnecessary and should have been avoided. It soon acquired greater importance to President Bush than the earlier and justifiable US military reaction to the attack launched by Al Qaeda from Afghanistan. That made the conflict in Afghanistan more prolonged, bloody, and eventually more complex geopolitically because of its increasing suction effect on Pakistan. Second, even earlier, the United States should not have neglected Afghanistan after the Soviets withdrew. The country was literally shattered and in desperate need of economic assistance to regain some measure of stability. Both the Bush I and Clinton administrations were passively indifferent. The resulting void was filled in the 1990s by the Taliban, backed by Pakistan, which sought thereby to gain geostrategic depth against India. Before long, the Taliban offered hospitality to Al Qaeda and the rest is history. After 9/11, the United States had no choice but to respond forcefully.

But even then, the United States could have sought to fashion a comprehensive strategy for isolating Al Qaeda's religiously extremist terrorists from the Muslim mainstream. That strategy, as this writer argued at the time on the op-ed pages of both the *Wall Street Journal* and the *New York Times,* should have combined an energetic campaign to disrupt existing terrorist networks (which the Bush administration, to its credit, did undertake) with a broader and longer-term political response designed to undercut support for terrorism by encouraging the moderates in the Muslim world to isolate Islamic extremism as an aberration, in a manner reminiscent of the successful political coalition against Saddam Hussein a decade earlier. But the pursuit of that strategic objective would have required also a serious US commitment to peace in the Middle East, and that proposition was anathema to Bush and his advisers.

The consequences were a dramatic decline in America's global standing in contrast to the last decade of the twentieth century, a progressive delegitimation of America's presidential and hence also national credibility, and a significant reduction in the self-identification of America's allies with America's security. The vast majority of US allies saw the 2003 war in Iraq as a unilateral, dubious, and expedient American overreaction to 9/11. Even in Afghanistan, where America's allies came to join America in a shared cause focused on Al Qaeda, their support wavered and gradually receded. Earlier than the Americans, NATO allies engaged in Afghanistan came to realize that Bush's conflating the campaign against Al Qaeda with the task of creating a modern and democratic Afghanistan was a contradiction in terms and in goals.

The fact is that modernizing reforms hastily introduced under foreign duress and in conflict with centuries of tradition rooted in deep religious convictions are not likely to endure without a protracted and assertive foreign presence. And the latter is likely to stimulate new spasms of resistance, not to mention the fact that the presence of about 14 million Pashtuns in Afghanistan (approximately 40% of its population) and about 28 million Pashtuns in Pakistan (about 15% of its population) makes more likely the eventual spread of the conflict from the former to the latter, thus resulting in an unmanageable territorial and demographic escalation.

The ominous lessons implicit in the foregoing are pertinent for America's near-term future. In addition to the unfinished business of Afghanistan, and even still of Iraq, America continues to confront in the vast, unstable, heavily populated region east of Suez and west of Xinjiang three potentially larger geopolitical dilemmas: the rise of Islamic fundamentalism in nuclear-armed Pakistan, the possibility of a direct conflict with Iran, and the probability that a US failure to promote an equitable Israeli-Palestinian peace accord will generate more intense popular hostility against America in the politically awakening Middle East.

In the meantime, America's basic strategic solitude persists, despite some cosmetic pronouncements by America's friends and some gestures of support from nominal regional partners. Not only are America's allies quietly disengaging from Afghanistan, but Afghanistan's three neighboring regional powers, themselves potentially threatened by a spreading Islamic extremism, are prudently passive. They maintain a formally cooperative posture of sympathy for America's concerns: in Russia's case, by providing some logistical assistance to US military efforts; in China's case, by reserved approval for sanctions against Iran; and in India's case, by modest economic assistance to Afghanistan. At the same time, their leading strategists are doubtless aware that America's continued embroilment in the region is diminishing America's global status even as it diverts potential threats to their countries' security. That, in a broad strategic calculus, is doubly beneficial to the still-resentful Russia, to the prudently rising China, and to the regionally anxious India. Both on regional as well as global scales, their geopolitical weight increases as America's global stature gradually diminishes.

Therefore, it is important that the American public and the US Congress fully digest the ominous reality that in addition to a political gridlock at home perpetuating America's domestic decay, a foreign policy not shaped by a realistic calculus of the national interest is a prescription for an America gravely at risk within the next twenty years. A larger war that spreads from Afghanistan to Pakistan, or a military collision with Iran, or even renewed hostilities between the Israelis and the Palestinians would draw America into regional conflicts with no clear-cut end in sight, with anti-American hostility spreading to the world of Islam as a whole, which accounts for about 25% of the world's total population. That would end any prospects of America exercising the hopeful world role that beckoned so uniquely a mere two decades ago.

As argued earlier, the United States retains the potential for genuine national renewal, but only if there is a mobilization of national will. The United States should also be able to undo the self-isolation and loss of influence produced by recent US foreign policies. Given the wide gap between US political and military power and that of any likely rival, a timely combination of determined national self-improvement and of broadly redefined strategic vision could still preserve America's global preeminence for a significant period.

But, it would be blithe escapism to dismiss entirely a much less positive vision of America's future. Three basic scenarios of how and when America's possible decline might occur come to mind. The extreme negative might involve a severe financial crisis suddenly plunging America and much of the world into a devastating depression. The close call that America experienced in 2007 is a reminder that such a dire scenario is not totally hypothetical. Coupled with the destructive consequences of an escalated US military engagement abroad, such a catastrophe could precipitate—in just several years—the end of America's global supremacy. It would be small comfort that the foregoing in all probability would be transpiring in the context of a generalized global upheaval, involving financial collapses, the explosive spread of global unemployment, political crises, the breakup of some ethnically vulnerable states, and rising violence on the part of the world's politically awakened and socially frustrated masses.

Though such a very rapid and historically drastic collapse by America may be less likely than a correction of US domestic and foreign policies (in part because 2007 was a valuable though painful warning signal), two other "intermediate" but alternative scenarios of continued decline might give rise to a much less gratifying future. The basic reality is this: America is simultaneously threatened by a slide backward into systemic obsolescence resulting from the lack of any forward progress on social, economic, and political reform and by the consequences of a misguided foreign policy that in recent years has been ominously out of touch with the postimperial age. Meanwhile, America's potential rivals (especially in some parts of Asia) attain, step by determined step, a mastery of twenty-first-century modernity. Before too long, some combination of the foregoing could prove fatal to America's domestic ideals as well as to its foreign interests.

Hence one "intermediate" and perhaps more likely outcome could involve a period of inconclusive domestic drift, combining spreading decay in America's quality of life, national infrastructure, economic competitiveness, and social well-being, though with some belated adjustments in US foreign policy somewhat reducing the high costs and painful risks of America's lately practiced propensity for lonely interventionism. Nonetheless, a deepening domestic stagnation would further damage America's global standing, undercut the credibility of US international commitments, and prompt other powers to undertake an increasingly urgent—but potentially futile—search for new arrangements to safeguard their financial stability and national security.

Conversely, America could recover at home and still fail abroad. Hence the other intermediate but still negative outcome could entail some moderate progress on the domestic front, but with the potential international benefits of the foregoing unfortunately vitiated by the cumulatively destructive consequences of continued and maybe even somewhat expanded solitary foreign adventures (e.g. in Pakistan or Iran). Success at home cannot compensate for a foreign policy that does not enlist and generate cooperation from others but instead engages the United States in lonely and draining campaigns against an increasing number of (at times self-generated) enemies. No success at home can be truly comprehensive if resources are wasted on debilitating foreign misadventures.

In either case, a steady and eventually even terminal decline in America's continued capacity to play a major world role would be the result. A lingering domestic or a protracted foreign malaise would sap America's vitality, progressively demoralize American society, reduce America's social appeal and global legitimacy, and produce perhaps by 2025 in an unsettled global setting a de facto end to America's hubristically once-proclaimed ownership of the twenty-first century. But who could then seek to claim it?

- PART 3 -

The World After America: By 2025, not Chinese but Chaotic

IF AMERICA FALTERS, THE WORLD IS UNLIKELY TO BE DOMINATED by a single preeminent successor, such as China. While a sudden and massive crisis of the American system would produce a fast-moving chain reaction leading to global political and economic chaos, a steady drift by America into increasingly pervasive decay and/or into endlessly widening warfare with Islam would be unlikely to produce, even by 2025, the "coronation" of an effective global successor. No single power will be ready by then to exercise the role that the world, upon the fall of the Soviet Union in 1991, expected the United States to play. More probable would be a protracted phase of rather inconclusive and somewhat chaotic realignments of both global and regional power, with no grand winners and many more losers, in a setting of international uncertainty and even of potentially fatal risks to global well-being. What follows analyzes the implications of that historically ominous—though certainly not predetermined—"if."

1: The Post-America Scramble

In the absence of a recognized leader, the resulting uncertainty is likely to increase tensions among competitors and inspire self-serving behavior. Thus, international cooperation is more likely to decline, with some powers seeking to promote exclusive regional arrangements as alternative frameworks of stability for the enhancement of their own interests. Historical contenders may vie more overtly, even with the use of force, for regional preeminence. Some weaker states may find themselves in serious jeopardy, as new power realignments emerge in response to major geopolitical shifts in the global distribution of power. The promotion of democracy might yield to the quest for enhanced national security based on varying fusions of authoritarianism, nationalism, and religion. The "global commons" could suffer from passive indifference or exploitation produced by a defensive concentration on narrower and more immediate national concerns.

Some key international institutions, such as the World Bank or the IMF, are already under increasing pressure from the rising, poorer, but highly populated states—with China and India in the forefront—for a general rearrangement of the existing distribution of voting rights, which is currently weighted toward the West. That distribution has already been challenged by some states in the G-20 as unfair. The obvious demand is that it should be based to a much greater degree on the actual populations of member states and less on their actual financial contributions. Such a demand, arising in the context of greater disorder and percolating unrest among the world's newly politically awakened peoples, could gain popularity among many as a step toward international (even though not domestic) democratization. And before long, the heretofore untouchable and almost seventy-year-old UN Security Council system of only five permanent members with exclusive veto rights may become widely viewed as illegitimate.

Even if a downward drift by America unfolds in a vague and contradictory fashion, it is likely that the leaders of the world's second-rank powers, among them Japan, India, Russia, and some EU members, are already assessing the potential impact of America's demise on their respective national interests. Indeed, the prospects of a post-America scramble may already be discreetly shaping the planning agenda of the chancelleries of the major foreign powers even if not yet dictating their actual policies. The Japanese, fearful of an assertive China dominating the Asian mainland, may be thinking of closer links with Europe. Leaders in India and Japan may well be considering closer political and even military cooperation as a hedge in case America falters and China rises. Russia, while perhaps engaging in wishful thinking (or even in schadenfreude) about America's uncertain prospects, may well have its eye on the independent states of the former Soviet Union as initial targets of its enhanced geopolitical influence. Europe, not yet cohesive, would likely be pulled in several directions: Germany and Italy toward Russia because of commercial interests, France and insecure Central Europe in favor of a politically tighter EU, and Great Britain seeking to manipulate a balance within the EU while continuing to preserve a special relationship with a declining United States. Others still may move more rapidly to carve out their own regional spheres: Turkey in the area of the old Ottoman Empire, Brazil in the Southern Hemisphere, and so forth.

None of the foregoing, however, have or are likely to have the requisite combination of economic, financial, technological, and military power to even consider inheriting America's leading role. Japan is dependent on the United States for military protection and would have to make the painful choice of accommodating China or perhaps of allying with India in joint opposition to it. Russia is still unable to come to terms with its loss of empire, is fearful of China's meteoric modernization, and is unclear as to whether it sees its future with Europe or in Eurasia. India's aspirations for major power status still tend to be measured by its rivalry with China. And Europe has yet to define itself politically while remaining conveniently dependent on American power. A genuinely cooperative effort by all of them to accept joint sacrifices for the sake of collective stability if America's power were to fade is not likely.

States, like individuals, are driven by inherited propensities—their traditional geopolitical inclinations and their sense of history—and they differ in their ability to discriminate between patient ambition and imprudent self-delusion. In reflecting on the possible consequences of a change in the global hierarchy of power in the first half of the twenty-first century, it may be useful therefore to remind oneself that in the twentieth century two extreme examples of impatient self-delusion resulted in national calamities. The most obvious was provided by Hitler's imprudent megalomania, which not only vastly overestimated Germany's global capacity for leadership but also prompted two personal strategic decisions that deprived him of any chance of retaining control even of continental Europe. The first, when already having conquered Europe but still at war with Great Britain, was to attack the Soviet Union; and the second was to declare war on the United States while still engaged in a mortal struggle with both the Soviet Union and Great Britain.

The second case was less dramatic but the stake was also global power. In the early 1960s the Soviet leadership proclaimed officially that it expected to surpass the United States during the decade of the 1980s in economic power and in technological capability (the ambitious Soviet claim was dramatized by its Sputnik success). Vastly overestimating its economic capabilities, by the late 1970s the USSR was pursuing an active arms race with the United States in which its technological capacity for innovation was central to the outcome, but in which its GNP limited the practical scope of its global political as well as military outreach. On both scores, the Soviet Union overreached disastrously. It then compounded the consequences of its miscalculation with the calamitous decision to invade Afghanistan in 1979. A decade later the exhausted Soviet Union ceased to exist and the Soviet bloc fragmented.

Today there is no equivalent to either Nazi Germany or Soviet Russia. No other major power in the current global pecking order manifests the failed self-delusion of the notorious twentieth-century aspirants to global power, and none as yet are politically, economically, or militarily ready to claim the mantle of global leadership—nor are any endowed with the vague but important quality of legitimacy that was still associated with America not so long ago. None proclaim to embody a doctrine of allegedly universal validity reinforced by claims of historical (in Hitler's case, one is even tempted to say "hysterical") determinism.

Most important, China, the state invariably mentioned as America's prospective successor, has an impressive imperial lineage and a strategic tradition of carefully calibrated patience, which have been critical to its overwhelmingly successful several-thousand-year-long history. China thus prudently accepts the existing international system, even if not viewing as permanent the prevailing hierarchy within it. It recognizes that its own success depends on the system not collapsing dramatically but instead evolving toward a gradual redistribution of power. It seeks more influence, craves international respect, and still resents its "century of humiliation," but increasingly feels self-confident about the future. Unlike the failed twentieth-century aspirants to world power, China's international posture is at this stage neither revolutionary nor messianic nor Manichean.

Moreover, the basic reality is that China is not yet—nor will it be for several more decades—ready to assume in full scope America's role in the world. Even China's leaders have repeatedly emphasized that in every important measure of development, wealth, and power—even several decades from now—China will still be a modernizing and developing state, significantly behind not only the United States but also Europe and Japan in the major per capita indexes of modernity and national power (see Figure 3.1).

China thus seems to understand—and its investments in America's well-being speak louder than words because they are based on self-interest—that a rapid decline of America's global primacy would produce a global crisis that could devastate China's own well-being and damage its long-range prospects. Prudence and patience are part of

FIGURE 3.1 POPULATION-AGING-GDP COMPARED

TOTAL POPULATION (MILLIONS)	US	EU	CHINA	JAPAN
1) Population 2010	317.64	497.53	1,354.15	127.00
2) Population 2025	358.74	506.22	1,453.14	120.79
3) Population 2030	369.98	505.62	1,462.47	117.42
4) Population 2050	403.93	493.86	1,417.05	101.66

SOURCES: UN projections, assuming medium fertility variant (EU is EU 27)

AGING — POPULATION 65+	US	EU	CHINA	JAPAN
1) % of Total Population 2010	13.0%	17.5%	8.2%	22.6%
2) % of Total Population 2025	18.1%	22.0%	13.4%	29.7%
3) % of Total Population 2030	19.8%	23.8%	15.9%	30.8%
4) % of Total Population 2050	21.6%	28.7%	23.3%	37.8%
5) Current Life Expectancy (years)	78.11	78.67	73.47	82.12

SOURCES: 5) CIA World Factbook; 1–4) UN projections, assuming medium fertility variant (EU is EU 27)

GDP (2005 $; NOT PPP)	US	EU	CHINA	JAPAN
1) GDP 2010 (2005 $ trillion)	$13.15	$14.63	$3.64	$4.54
2) GDP 2025 (2005 $ trillion)	$19.48	$19.10	$16.12	$5.56
3) GDP 2030 (2005 $ trillion)	$22.26	$20.34	$21.48	$5.79
4) GDP 2050 (2005 $ trillion)	$38.65	$26.62	$46.27	$6.22
5) GDP Per Capita 2010 (2005 $)	$42,372	$29,649	$2,699	$35,815
6) GDP Per Capita 2025 (2005 $)	$54,503	$38,320	$11,096	$47,163
7) GDP Per Capita 2030 (2005 $)	$59,592	$40,901	$14,696	$50,965
8) GDP Per Capita 2050 (2005 $)	$88,029	$55,763	$32,486	$66,361

SOURCE: Carnegie Endowment for International Peace's The World Order in 2050, February 2010

China's imperial DNA. But China is also ambitious, proud, and conscious that its unique history is but a prologue to its destiny. No wonder then that in a burst of candor an astute Chinese public figure, who obviously had concluded that America's decline and China's rise were both inevitable, not long ago soberly noted to a visiting American: "But, please, let America not decline too quickly. . . ."

Accordingly, the Chinese leaders have been prudently restrained in laying any overt claims to global leadership. By and large, they are still guided by Deng Xiaoping's famous maxim: "Observe calmly; secure our position: cope with affairs calmly; hide our capacities and bide our time; be good at maintaining a low profile, and never claim leadership." That cautious and even deceptive posture happens also to be in keeping with the ancient strategic guidance of Sun Tzu who compellingly argued that the wisest posture in combat is to lay back, let one's opponent make fatal mistakes, and only then capitalize on them. China's official attitude toward America's domestic travails and foreign adventures is suggestively reminiscent of that strategic guidance. Beijing's historical confidence goes hand in hand with its calculated prudence and long-term ambitions.

It is also relevant to note that China—despite its singular domestic achievements—has until recently not sought to universalize its experience. It no longer propounds—as it did under Mao during its extremist Communist phase—ambitious notions regarding the unique historical validity for all of mankind of its progress toward modernity nor posits doctrinaire claims of the allegedly higher morality of its social arrangements. Its global calling card stresses instead one very prosaic but practical and widely envied theme: China's remarkable GDP annual growth rate. That appealing message gives China a significant competitive edge, especially in Latin America and in underdeveloped Africa, as it seeks to increase its investments without pressing for political reforms. (For example, China-Africa trade grew 1000% from $10 billion in 2000 to $107 billion in 2008.)

In addition to taking into account China's outlook and traditional conduct, note must be taken of the fact that some potentially major uncertainties hover over China's own internal political and social development. Politically, the state has evolved from a radical form of totalitarianism—periodically punctuated by ruthlessly brutal and even bloody mass campaigns (most notably the Great Leap Forward and the Cultural Revolution)—to an increasingly nationalistic authoritarianism in charge of state capitalism. So far, the new formula has been a spectacular economic success. But its social underpinnings could prove to be fragile. As noted earlier, China's economic growth and rise in social well-being has already generated sharp social disparities that can no longer be hidden from public sight. The new middle class in the major cities has gained not only a measure of prosperity but also unprecedented access—despite official efforts to constrain it—to global information. Such access does stimulate new political and social expectations. It also produces resentments over existing limitations to political rights and breeds individuals willing even to take risks as active political dissidents.

Such dissidents have a potentially huge clientage especially as the more privileged middle class is beginning to aspire to a freer political dialogue, a more open social critique, and more direct access to national policy making. Economic dissatisfaction is also beginning to surface among the much more numerous industrial workers and among the even more numerous peasants. The millions of Chinese industrial workers are just beginning to realize how underpaid they have been in comparison to the increasingly prosperous new middle class. The even larger masses of genuinely poor peasantry—some of whom make up the scores of millions of semi-unemployed workers free floating from city to city in search of menial work—are only beginning to develop their own aspirations for a larger share of China's national wealth.

China's preoccupation with its internal stability is thus likely to increase. A serious domestic political or social crisis, such as a repeat of Tiananmen Square in 1989, could do major damage to China's international standing and set back the undeniable accomplishments of the last three decades. That consideration is likely to incline the Chinese leadership to remain discreet regarding a timetable for China's more rapid ascent on the global pecking order. And yet they must also take into account the growing national pride among China's elite, especially vis-à-vis the United States. Indeed, toward the end of the first decade of the twenty-first century semiofficial Chinese commentators (notably contributors to *Liaowang*, the weekly general affairs journal published by China's official news agency) began to question more openly the overall historical legitimacy of the existing global status quo. Some Chinese observers of international affairs even began to postulate what could be the beginning for a doctrinal claim of the universal validity of the Chinese model. As one contributor put it:

> The malfunctioning of the international mechanism today is the malfunctioning of the Western model dominated by the "American model." At a deeper level, it is the malfunctioning of Western culture. Even as it actively participates in global governance and properly fulfills its role as a large developing country, China should take the initiative to disseminate the Chinese concept of "harmony" around the world. In the course of world history, a country's rise is often accompanied by the birth of a new concept. The concept of "harmony" is a theoretical expression of China's peaceful rise and should be transmitted to the world along with the concepts of justice, win-win, and joint development.[1]

Chinese commentators at times also became more outspoken in their direct criticisms of America's global leadership. Thus another Chinese foreign affairs commentator asserted:

> Though the United States' "single-pole" ambition was seriously set back by the financial crisis, it does not accept the

> multi-polar international structure, still tries hard to maintain its world hegemony, and tries by all possible means to safeguard its status as "the primary leader." With China's continuous rapid rise and the elevation of its status as a rising big power, the "sequence" of the power "ranking list" between China and the United States will change sooner or later, and it will be unavoidable that the two sides will contend for their ranking positions. . . The international financial crisis exposed the defects of the "American model," so the United States increased its effort to "block" and disparage the "Chinese model" in the international community. The differences between the political systems and values of the two countries may be further "magnified."[2]

Particularly since the financial crisis of 2007, Chinese criticisms of the American system and of America's global posture have become frequent and outspoken. America has been blamed for precipitating the financial crisis of 2007 and of failing to appreciate the vital Chinese role in developing a collective international response to it. The Chinese political media have also taken America to task with increasing severity for its alleged insensitivity to China's interests and for injecting itself in 2010 into China's dispute with its Asian neighbors concerning their prospective rights in the South China Sea. Some commentators even accused America of seeking to encircle China.

Such reactions reflect not only a rising historical self-confidence on the part of China—a confidence that could easily become overconfidence—but also a more assertive Chinese nationalism. Chinese nationalism is a potent and potentially explosive force. Though deeply rooted in historical pride, it is also driven by resentment over past but not-so-distant humiliations. It can be channeled and exploited by those in power. Indeed, in the event of internal social disruptions, the appeal of nationalism could become the expedient source of social cohesion for the preservation of the political status quo.

At some stage, however, it could also damage China's global image, at some cost to its international interests. A highly nationalistic and assertive China—boastful of its rising power—could unintentionally mobilize a powerful coalition of neighbors against itself. The fact is that none of China's important neighbors—Japan, India, and Russia—are ready to acknowledge China's entitlement to America's place on the global totem pole if it becomes vacant. Perhaps China's neighbors might eventually have no choice, but they almost certainly would first maneuver against such an ascension. They might even be inclined to seek support from a waning America in order to offset an overly assertive China. The resulting scramble could become regionally intense, especially given the somewhat similar susceptibility among these three major neighbors of China toward passionate nationalisms of their own.

Even an informal anti-Chinese coalition of Japan, India, and Russia thus would have serious geopolitical implications for China. Unlike America's favorable geographic location, China is potentially vulnerable to a strategic encirclement. Japan stands in the way of China's access to the Pacific Ocean, Russia separates China from Europe, and India towers over an ocean named after itself that serves as China's main access to the Middle East. So far "a peacefully rising China" (so self-described by Chinese leaders) has been gaining friends and even dependencies in Asia, but an assertively nationalistic China could find itself more isolated.

A phase of acute international tensions in Asia could then ensue. Such tensions could assume dangerous manifestations, particularly in the case of the developing China-India rivalry in South Asia specifically, but also in Asia as a whole more generally. Indian strategists speak openly of a greater India exercising a dominant position in an area ranging from Iran to Thailand. India is also positioning itself to control the Indian Ocean militarily; its naval and air power programs point clearly in that direction—as do politically guided efforts to establish for India strong positions, with geostrategic implications, in adjoining Bangladesh and Burma. India's involvement in the construction of port

MAP 3.1 THE 'ENCIRCLEMENT' OF CHINA

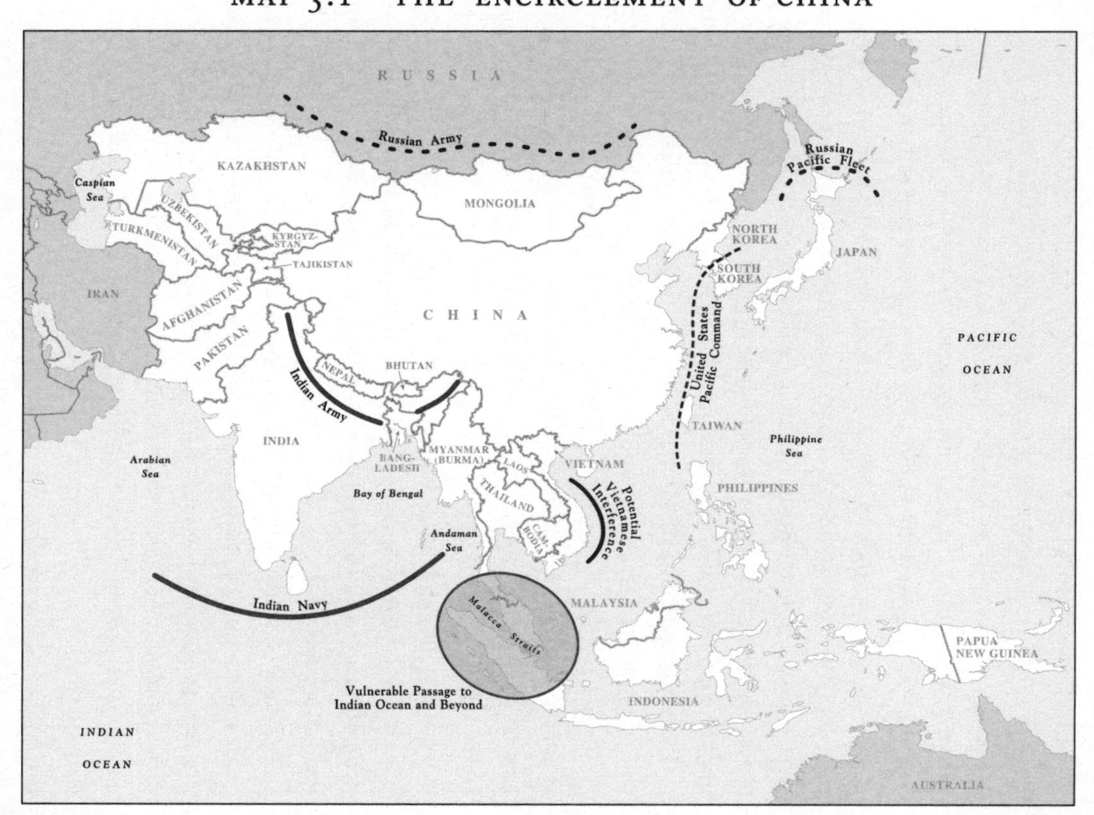

facilities in these two states enhances India's ability eventually to seek control over maritime passage through the Indian Ocean.

China's strategic relationship with Pakistan as well as its efforts to match India's presence in Burma and Bangladesh also reflect a larger strategic design as well as an understandable intent to protect its essential maritime access through the Indian Ocean to the Middle East from the whims of a powerful neighbor. The Chinese have been exploring the possibility of building a major facility in Pakistan's southwestern coast near Iran, at Gwadar, a peninsula jutting into the Indian Ocean, and connecting it by road or pipeline with China. In Burma, where India has been upgrading the port of Sittwe in order to obtain a shortcut to its geographically inaccessible northeast, the Chinese have been investing in the port of Kyauk Phru, from which a pipeline to China could also be built, thereby reducing Chinese dependence on a much longer passage through the Strait of Malacca. Political-military influence in Burma itself has been the larger stake involved in these geopolitically significant undertakings.

China, moreover, has a vital interest in Pakistan remaining a serious military complication for India's strategic interests and growing aspirations. The Chinese desire to construct a naval facility in Pakistan was thus not only designed to establish a Chinese presence in the Indian Ocean but also to signal the importance that China assigns to a viable Pakistan and to a healthy Sino-Pakistan relationship. Though China and India have been careful to avoid a military clash since their brief collision in 1962, China's engagement with Pakistan, Pakistan's internal vulnerability, India's and China's naval competition in the Indian Ocean, and both nations' rising global status could trigger a dangerous arms race or, even worse, a real conflict. Fortunately, so far, the leaders of both countries have shown that they recognize that a minor war would resolve nothing while a major war between the two nuclear powers could destroy everything.

Nonetheless, even some border incidents could generate intense Chinese and/or Indian nationalistic passions that would be difficult to control politically. In that respect, India could prove to be more volatile, because its political system is less authoritarian and the Indian public's understandable fear of Chinese-Pakistani collusion makes it more susceptible to aroused anti-Chinese feelings than is the case with anti-Indian mass sentiments in China. Moreover, the Indian press—reflecting resentment of China's much more impressive modernization, more productive economy, and higher global standing—has become increasingly explicit in publicizing China's potential geopolitical threat to India's security. India's second-largest English-language daily read by its English-speaking elite thus interpreted for its readers the reciprocal Indian-Chinese rivalry in South Asia just described above:

> China's calculated and motivated war preparation is for whom? . . . China built Gwadar port in Pakistan's critically sensitive location to have her footprint in controlling sea-lanes and also watching India. . . . Thus with covert and overt support from Pakistan, China succeeded in neutralizing India through land and sea. Apart from that, violating all international rules, China outright changed Pakistan into a nuclear powered country, to counter India. Moreover, China's move to build ports, oil pipelines, and highways in Myanmar too, is not less significant. Added to this, the Hambentola port built with Chinese assistance in Sri Lanka, which is physically a detached part of the Indian landmass is a well planned execution of China's "String of Pearls Strategy" to encircle India across the Indian Ocean.[3]

It would be historically ironic, indeed, if the reemergence of China on the world scene resulted in conflicts to the detriment of Asia's rising role in world affairs. But China's rise so far has been impressive in its tangible accomplishments and somewhat reassuring in its calculated international conduct. Top Chinese political leaders appear to realize that China's long-term ambitions could also be the victim of a global plunge into a post-America scramble.

In any case, irrespective of the calculations of top Chinese leaders and some symptoms of rising nationalistic impatience, it does appear that China's ascent to global preeminence might encounter considerably more obstacles than was the case with America's rise, and if pursued with evident impatience it could generate more active opposition than America ever had to confront during its ascendancy. China does not enjoy the advantages of America's favorable geographical and historical circumstances at its takeoff stage in the early twentieth century. And unlike America's emergence as the sole global superpower in the last decade of the twentieth century, China's current rise is taking place in the context not only of rivalry with other regional powers but it is also highly dependent on the continued stability of the existing international economic system. Yet that very system could be in jeopardy if a post-America scramble generates a worldwide inclination toward a short-term but intense assertion of national interests at a time when the need for global cooperation is greater than ever.

2: The Geopolitically Most Endangered States

In the contemporary world, the security of a number of weaker states located geographically next to major regional powers depends (even in the absence of specific US commitments to some of them) on the international status quo reinforced by America's global preeminence. The states in that vulnerable position are today's geopolitical equivalents of nature's "most endangered species." Some of them have also come to be viewed by their more powerful neighbors as symbols of resented American intrusion into their existing or claimed regional spheres of influence. Accordingly, the temptation to act assertively toward them would rise in proportion to the decline in America's global status.

While the existing major regional powers may resent that American role, they have a stake in not precipitating a chain reaction that causes the international system itself to break down. It was the possibility of such a chain reaction that constrained Russia in 2008 from crushing Georgia (during the brief Russo-Georgian collision over Ossetia and Abkhazia). Russia realized that its continued military operations could damage East-West relations in general and perhaps lead to some sort of a confrontation with the United States. Given its relative weakness, and the relatively unsatisfactory performance of its conventional forces, it decided to halt what could have become a pyrrhic victory and to settle for a minor territorial success. But an America in serious decline for domestic and/or external reasons would almost automatically reduce such inherent restraint. The cumulative result would be a wide-ranging drift toward an international reality characterized by the survival of the strongest.

A partial listing of the more vulnerable states, with brief comments, now follows (its sequence implies neither level of vulnerability nor geopolitical probability):

Georgia

An American decline would leave Georgia totally vulnerable to both Russian political intimidation and military aggression. The United States currently supports Georgian sovereignty and endorses Georgia's quest to join NATO. The United States has also provided Georgia with $3 billion in aid since 1991, with $1 billion of that assistance coming in the aftermath of the 2008 war. The foregoing has been underscored by the official assertion that "the United States does not recognize spheres of influence."[4]

America's decline would obviously affect the credibility of such general commitments. The resulting limitations on American capabilities—especially those affecting NATO's willingness to stand firm—could by itself stir Russian desires to reclaim its old sphere of influence, because of the diminished US presence in Europe, regardless of the state of US-Russian relations. An additional factor motivating the Kremlin would be the intense personal hatred nourished by Vladimir Putin toward current Georgian President Mikhail Saakashvili, whose removal from power has become something of an obsession for the Russian leader.

A further consideration motivating Russia could be the fact that the United States sponsored the development through Georgia of the southern corridor of energy supply to Europe, especially the existing Baku-Tbilisi-Ceyhan oil pipeline and the Baku-Tbilisi-Erzurum gas pipeline that is eventually going to reach Europe through Turkey. Russia would reap an enormous geopolitical as well as economic benefit from reclaiming its near monopoly over energy routes to Europe if the US ties to Georgia were severed.

Georgia's subordination to Russia would likely lead to a domino effect on Azerbaijan. Azerbaijan is the key supplier to the southern corridor and thus to Europe's energy diversification, which indirectly limits Russian political influence in European affairs. Thus in the case of an American decline, Russia, particularly if emboldened by a successful effort to control Georgia, would most likely use its greater freedom of action to intimidate Azerbaijan. And in such circumstances, Azerbaijan would not be inclined to defy a reinvigorated Russia. Europe at large would thus be under greater pressure to accommodate Russia's political agenda.

Taiwan

Since 1972, the United States has formally accepted the PRC's "one China" postulate, as outlined in three Sino-American communiqués (1972, 1979, and 1982), while maintaining that neither side shall alter the status quo by force. A peaceful "status quo" has been the basis for American cross-straits policy, since a relationship both with a growing China and an increasingly democratic and free market–oriented Taiwan is beneficial to a strong US presence in the Pacific and to American business interests in the Far East.

The United States justifies its continued arms sales to Taiwan by stating that it is part of its status quo policy, confirmed in 1979 at the time of the US-China normalization of diplomatic relations, and that updated Taiwanese defense capabilities are necessary for the protection of Taiwan's autonomy until such time as the issue of Taiwan is resolved peacefully. China rejects that position and reserves on the grounds of sovereignty the right to use force. However, in the meantime it has been increasingly pursuing a policy of cross-straits accommodation. In recent years, Taiwan and China have been improving their relationship, signing the Economic Cooperation Framework Agreement (ECFA) on relatively equal terms in the summer of 2010.

America's decline would obviously increase Taiwan's vulnerability. Decision makers in Taipei could then neither ignore direct Chinese pressure nor the sheer attraction of an economically successful China. That, at the very least, would speed up the timetable for cross-straits reunification, but on unequal terms favoring the mainland. And if America's decline in the meantime adversely affected the strategic connection between the United States and Japan, China could even be tempted—especially given the depth of Chinese national feelings about the matter—to reinforce its pressures on Taiwan with the threat to use force in order to effect the "one China" that the United States accepted as a political reality back in 1972. A politically successful threat to that effect could prompt a general crisis of confidence in Japan and South Korea regarding the reliability of existing American commitments.

South Korea

The United States signed a Mutual Defense Pact with South Korea in 1953 and has been the guarantor of South Korea's security ever since the 1950 attack on it by North Korea, with Soviet and Chinese collusion. Additionally, South Korea's remarkable economic takeoff and democratic political system has been a testimonial to the success of US engagement in South Korea. But over the years, the North Korean regime has staged a number of provocations against South Korea, ranging from assassinations of its cabinet members to attempts to kill the

South Korean president. In 2010, the North Koreans sank a South Korean warship, the *Cheonan,* killing much of its crew; and in November 2010 North Korea shelled a South Korean island, killing some soldiers and civilians. In each case, South Korea looked to America for assistance, underlining the degree to which South Korea continues to rely on the United States for its physical security.

North Korea has also been altering its military strategy to emphasize the possibility of asymmetrical warfare against South Korea, based on its development of short-range ballistic missiles, long-range artillery, and nuclear weapons. South Korea has the means to resist a conventional attack from North Korea, but it is heavily reliant on its alliance with the United States to deter and defend against a comprehensive attack.

A US decline would confront South Korea with painful choices: either to accept Chinese regional dominance and rely further on China to act as the guarantor of security in East Asia, or to seek a much stronger, though historically unpopular, relationship with Japan, because of their shared democratic values and fear of aggression from the Democratic People's Republic of Korea or China. But Japan's inclination to stand up to China without strong US backing is problematical at best. Thus South Korea could face a military or political threat on its own, if US security commitments in East Asia became less credible.

Belarus

Twenty years after the fall of the Soviet Union, Belarus remains politically and economically dependent on Russia. One-third of all its exports go to Russia while Belarus is almost entirely dependent on Russia for its energy needs. Moreover, a majority of Belarus's 9.6 million people speak Russian, Belarus as a national state has been independent only since 1991, and the depth of its people's national identity has not been tested—all of which are factors that preserve Moscow's influence. For example, in 2009, the Russian army held major maneuvers (with

Belarusian participation) in Belarus designated as Zapad (i.e., "the West") in which it repelled a hypothetical Western attack, culminating with a simulated Russian nuclear attack on the capital of a bordering Western (i.e., NATO) state.

Nonetheless, Belarus's dependent relationship with Russia has not been without conflict. Belarus has not recognized South Ossetia and Abkhazia as independent states (which Moscow established after its clash in 2008 with Georgia) despite open pressures by Putin. At the same time, its lack of a democratic process, as manifested in the seventeen-year-long dictatorship exercised by President Lukashenko, has stood in the way of any meaningful relations with the West. Poland, Sweden, and Lithuania have been trying to develop some civic connections between Belarus and the EU, but with very limited progress.

Consequently, a marked decline by America would give Russia a largely riskless opportunity to absorb Belarus, with at most a minimal use of force, and with little other cost beyond its reputation as a responsible regional power. Unlike the case of Georgia, Belarus would have neither Western arms nor enjoy the West's political sympathy. The EU would be unlikely to respond in the absence of American support, and some Western European countries would likely be indifferent to the cause of Belarus. The UN, in such circumstances, would be largely passive. The Central European states, all too aware of the dangers of an emboldened Russia, might demand a common NATO response, but with America in decline it is unlikely that they could muster a collective and forceful reaction.

Ukraine

Russia's absorption of Belarus, without too much cost or pain, would jeopardize the future of Ukraine as a genuinely sovereign state. Ukraine's relationship with Russia, since gaining its independence in 1991, has been as prone to tension as its relationship with the West has been prone to indecision. Russia has repeatedly tried to coerce Ukraine into adopting policies beneficial to Russia, using energy as a political tool. In 2005, 2007, and 2009, Russia has either threatened or actually stopped oil and gas flow to Ukraine because of price issues and Ukraine's outstanding energy debt. In the summer of 2010, Ukraine's President Yanukovych was pressured to agree to an extension of Russia's lease of a naval base in the Ukrainian Black Sea port of Sevastopol for another twenty-five years in exchange for a preferential pricing of Russian energy deliveries to Ukraine.

Ukraine is a significant European state of some 45 million people, with a strong industry and potentially very productive agriculture. A union with Russia would both enrich Russia and represent a giant step toward the restoration of its imperial sphere, a matter of much nostalgia to some of its leaders. Hence it is likely that the Kremlin will continue to press Ukraine to join a "common economic space" with Russia, gradually stripping Ukraine of direct control over its major industrial assets through mergers and takeovers by Russian firms. At the same time, quiet efforts will go on to infiltrate the Ukrainian security services and military command, in order to weaken Ukraine's ability to protect, when need be, its sovereignty.

Eventually—assuming America's decline—a passive European response to the absorption of Belarus, not to mention an earlier and successful use of force to intimidate Georgia, could entice the Russian leaders to attempt at some point a more overt reunification. But it would be a very complicated undertaking, perhaps requiring the use of some force and at least a contrived economic crisis within Ukraine to make a formal union with an economically more resilient Russia more palatable to the Ukrainians. Russia would still risk provoking a belated nationalist reaction, especially from the Ukrainian-speaking west and center of the country. With the passage of time, Ukraine as a nation-state is gaining a deeper emotional commitment from a younger generation—whether primarily Ukrainian or Russian speaking—that increasingly views Ukrainian statehood as normal and as part of its identity. Hence time may not be working in favor of a voluntary submission by Kyiv to Moscow, but impatient Russian pressures to that end as well as the West's indifference could generate a potentially explosive situation on the very edge of the European Union.

Afghanistan

Devastated by nine years of extraordinarily brutal warfare waged by the Soviet Union, ignored by the West for a decade after the Soviet withdrawal, mismanaged by the medieval Taliban rulers who seized power with Pakistani assistance, and exposed during the Bush presidency to seven years of halfhearted US military operations and sporadic economic assistance, Afghanistan is a country in shambles. It has little economic output outside of its illegal narcotics trade, with 40% unemployment and a global ranking of 219th in GDP per capita. Only 15–20% of Afghans have access to electricity.

The most likely results of a rapid US disengagement brought on by war fatigue or the early effects of an American decline would be internal disintegration and an external power play among nearby states for influence in Afghanistan. In the absence of an effective and stable government in Kabul, the country would be dominated by rival warlords. Both Pakistan and India would more assertively and openly compete for influence in Afghanistan—with Iran also probably involved. As the result, the possibility of at least an indirect war between India and Pakistan would increase.

Iran would likely try to exploit the Pakistani-Indian rivalry in seeking advantage for itself. Both India and Iran fear that any increase in Pakistani influence in Afghanistan would severely affect the regional balance of power, and in India's case compound the belligerent stance of Pakistan. In addition, adjoining central Asian states—given the presence of significant Tadjik, Uzbek, Kirghiz, and Turkmen communities in Afghanistan—could become involved in the regional power play as well. And the more players involved in Afghanistan, the more likely it is that a larger regional conflict could break out.

Second, even if a solid Afghan government is in place at the time of currently planned American disengagement—with some semblance of central control—a subsequent failure to sustain US-sponsored international involvement in the region's stability is likely to reignite the embers of ethnic and religious passions. The Taliban could reemerge as the major disruptive force in Afghanistan—with help from the Pakistani Taliban—and/or Afghanistan could descend into a state of tribal warlordism. Afghanistan then could become a still larger player in the international drug trade, and even perhaps again a haven for international terrorism.

Pakistan

While Pakistan is armed with twenty-first-century nuclear weapons and is held together by a professional late twentieth-century army, the majority of its people—despite a politically active middle class and a congested urban population—are still premodern, rural, and largely defined by regional and tribal identities. Together they share the Muslim faith, which provided the passionate impulse for a separate state upon Britain's departure from India. The resulting conflicts with India have defined Pakistan's sense of separate national identity, while the forcible division of Kashmir has sustained a shared and profound antipathy for each other.

Pakistan's political instability is its greatest vulnerability. And a decline in US power would reduce America's ability to aid Pakistan's consolidation and development. Pakistan could transform into a state run by the military, or a radical Islamic state, or a state that combines both military and Islamic rule, or a "state" with no centralized government at all. The worst-case scenarios are that Pakistan devolves into some variation of nuclear warlordism or transforms into a militant-Islamic and anti-Western government similar to Iran. The latter could in turn infect Central Asia, generating wider regional instability of concern both to Russia and to China.

In the above circumstances, America's decline would also increase Chinese security concerns about South Asia and could intensify Indian temptations to undermine Pakistan. China's exploitation of any clashes between Pakistan and India would also be more likely, thus potentially increasing regional instability. Ultimately, an unstable peace or a wider conflict in the region would depend almost entirely on the degree to which both India and China could restrain their own increasingly nationalistic impulses to exploit Pakistan's instability in order to gain the regional upper hand.

Israel and the Greater Middle East

In addition to specific states becoming immediately endangered, one also needs to take into account the more general probability that America's decline would set in motion tectonic shifts undermining the political stability of the entire Middle East. Though in varying degrees, all the states in the region remain vulnerable to internal populist pressures, social unrest, and religious fundamentalism, as seen in the events of early 2011. If America's decline were to occur with the Israeli-Palestinian conflict still unresolved, the failure to implement by then a mutually acceptable two-state solution would further inflame the region's political atmosphere. Regional hostility to Israel would then intensify.

It is reasonable to assume that perceived American weakness would at some point tempt the more powerful states in the region, notably Iran or Israel, to preempt anticipated dangers. In these circumstances even cautious jockeying for tactical advantage could precipitate eruptions of local violence—say, involving Hamas or Hezbollah, backed by Iran, versus Israel—which could then escalate into wider and more bloody military encounters as well as new intifadas. Weak entities such as Lebanon and Palestine would then pay an especially high price in civilian death tolls. Even worse, such conflicts could rise to truly horrific levels through strikes and counterstrikes between Iran and Israel.

The latter turn of events could then draw the United States into a direct confrontation with Iran. Since a conventional war would not be a favorable option for an America fatigued by the wars in Iraq and Afghanistan (and by then perhaps also in Pakistan), the United States presumably would rely on its air supremacy to inflict painful strategic damage on Iran, and especially on its nuclear facilities. The resulting human toll would infuse into Iranian nationalism a lasting hostility toward America while further blending Islamic fundamentalism with Iranian nationalism. Islamic radicalism and extremism in the Middle East at large would also be inflamed, with potentially damaging consequences for the world economy. Under these circumstances, Russia would obviously benefit economically from the rise in the price of energy and politically from the concentration of Islamic passions on the United States as Muslim grievances shifted away from Russia. Turkey might become more overtly sympathetic to the Islamic sense of victimhood, and China could gain a freer hand in pursuing its own interests in the area.

In that geopolitical context, and contrary to those who believe that Israel's long-term security would benefit from an America locked into a hostile relationship with the world of Islam, Israel's long-term survival could be placed in jeopardy. Israel has the military capacity and the national will to repel immediate dangers to itself, and also to repress the Palestinians. But America's long-standing and generous support for Israel, derived more from a genuine sense of moral obligation and less from real strategic congruity, could become less reliable. The inclination to disengage from the region could grow as America declines, despite public support for Israel, while much of the world would probably blame America for the regional upheaval. With the Arab masses politically aroused and more inclined to engage in prolonged violence ("people's war"), an Israel that could become internationally viewed—to cite Deputy Prime Minister Ehud Barak's ominous warning in 2010—as an "apartheid" state would have doubtful long-term prospects.

The vulnerability of the US–supported Persian Gulf states would also be likely to intensify. As US power in the region recedes and as Iran continues its military buildup and pursues greater influence in Iraq—which prior to the 2003 US invasion stood as a bulwark to Iranian expansion—uncertainty and insecurity within Saudi Arabia, Kuwait, Bahrain, Qatar, Oman, and the UAE are likely to intensify. They may have to seek new and more effective protectors of their security. China would be an obvious and potentially economically motivated candidate, thereby altering dramatically the geopolitical configuration of the Middle East.

Just thirty-five years ago, the United States benefited from strong relationships with the four most important countries in the Middle East: Iran, Saudi Arabia, Egypt, and Turkey. As a result, American interests in the region were secure. Today, American influence with each of these four states is largely reduced. America and Iran are locked in a hostile relationship; Saudi Arabia is critical of America's evolving regional policy; Turkey is disappointed by the lack of American understanding for its regional ambitions; and Egypt's rising skepticism regarding its relationship with Israel is setting it at odds with America's priorities. In brief, the US position in the Middle East is manifestly deteriorating. An American decline would end it.

Unlike its impact on the especially vulnerable countries, America's slide into international impotence or even into a paralyzing crisis would not significantly affect the scale of international terrorist activity. Most acts of terrorism are—and have been—domestic, not international. Whether in Italy, where in 1978 some 2,000 terrorist acts occurred in a single year, or in contemporary Pakistan, where the casualties from terrorist killings annually measure in the high hundreds and where high-level assassinations are commonplace, the sources and targets of domestic terrorism have been the product of internal conditions. This has been true for over a hundred years, since political terrorism first appeared as a significant phenomenon in late nineteenth-century Russia and France. Therefore, a precipitous decline in American power would not influence the scale of terrorist activities in, for example, India because their occurrence in the first place relates little to America's role in the world. Because most domestic terrorism is rooted in radicalized local or regional political tensions, only changing local conditions can affect the scale of this type of terrorism.

America has become the target of a genuinely global brand of terrorist activity only over the past decade and a half. Its rise is associated with the populist passions that have grown because of political awakening, particularly in some Muslim states. America has become the target of terrorism because Islamic religious extremists have focused their intense hatred on America as the enemy of Islam and as the neocolonialist "great Satan." Osama bin Laden used the notion of America as the embodiment of Satan to justify his 2001 fatwah, which led to the September 11 terrorist assaults on the United States. Further justification for the targeting of America by Al Qaeda has been the alleged desecration of sacred Islamic sites by the US military deployments in Saudi Arabia and by America's support for Israel. Bruce Riedel, Senior Fellow at the Saban Center of the Brookings Institution in Washington, has observed that bin Laden in twenty of his twenty-four major speeches, both before and after 9/11, justified violence against America by citing its support for Israel.

The inspiration for these international terrorist acts has been the Manichean view of the United States held by extremist Muslim fanatics. Accordingly, an American decline would not serve to dissuade these groups. Nor would it serve to empower them because their message lacks the distinctly political aspects of other domestically entrenched groups like Hamas and Hezbollah. It is thus doubtful that such fundamentalist terrorism can gain control over the ongoing upheavals in the Islamic world. And even if it did, it is more likely to result in internecine struggles than in any united action against outside states. It is also noteworthy that in the years from Bakunin* to Bin Laden, nowhere has terrorism achieved its political objective or succeeded in replacing states as the principal actor per se on the international stage. Terrorism can intensify international turmoil but it cannot define its substance.

In addition, the foregoing discussion points to the following more general conclusions:

First, the existing international system is likely to become increasingly incapable of preventing conflicts once it becomes evident that America is unwilling or unable to protect states it once considered, for national interest and/or doctrinal reasons, worthy of its engagement. Furthermore, once awareness of that new reality becomes internationally pervasive, a more widespread tendency toward regional violence, in which stronger states become more unilateral in their treatment of weaker neighbors, may ensue. Serious threats to peace are likely to originate from major regional powers inclined to settle geopolitical or ethnic scores with their immediate but much weaker neighbors. The fading of American power would create an open space for such an assertion of force, with relatively little short-term cost to its initiator.

Second, several of the previous scenarios represent the unfinished legacy of the Cold War. They are a testament to America's lost opportunity to use the consolidation of a peaceful zone of security near Russia to engage Russia in closer security cooperation. That might even have involved a joint NATO-Russia treaty as NATO was expanding, thereby furthering a more enduring East-West accommodation while helping to consolidate Russia's nascent democracy.[5] Perhaps such an initiative by the West would have been rebuffed, but it was never explored. Instead,

* Mikhail Bakunin, born in Russia in 1814, was the central figure in nineteenth-century Anarchism and a prominent Russian advocate of terrorism. His disagreement with Karl Marx led to the schism between the anarchist and Marxist wings of the revolutionary socialist movement.

after 2001 the United States became obsessed with its "war on terror" and with gathering support for its military campaigns in Iraq and Afghanistan to the detriment of any larger geostrategic designs. Meanwhile, Russia became focused on the establishment of a more repressive authoritarianism and on the restoration of its own influence in the space of the former Soviet bloc.

Third, East Asia and South Asia would be the regions most vulnerable to international conflicts in a post-American world. The rise both of China and of India as major regional powers with global aspirations is prompting shifts in the region's distribution of power while their evident rivalry is generating unavoidable uncertainties. If America falters, weaker countries may be forced to make geopolitical choices in a setting of increasing instability even if China and India avoid a major collision. At the same time, pressure is rising in China for a pushback of US power in Asia while concern is growing in East and Southeast Asia over China's potentially expansionist aspirations. Creating even more uncertainty is the reality of North Korea's openly proclaimed quest for nuclear weapons in the context of internal political dynamics that are as undecipherable as they are dangerously unpredictable. America's decline would diminish an external restraint that states considering the unilateral use of force normally have to take into account. In brief, America's decline would inevitably contribute to a rise in the frequency, scope, and intensity of regional conflicts.

3: The End of a Good Neighborhood

America is bordered by only two states, Mexico and Canada. Though both are good neighbors, Mexico poses a much more serious risk for America in the event of American decline because of its far more volatile political and economic conditions. For example, America and Canada share an enormous but mostly tranquil border, while the US-Mexico border, though much smaller, is the site of violence, ethnic tension, drug and weapons trafficking, illegal immigration, and political demonization. And, though both Mexico and Canada are economically dependent on the United States, with relatively similar GDPs, roughly 15% of Mexico's labor force works inside America and Mexico's percentage of population below the poverty line is more than double that of Canada. Furthermore, Mexico's internal political dynamics are much more unstable and its relationship with the United States has been historically more turbulent. Therefore, while Canada would be adversely affected by an American decline, Mexico would likely plunge into a messy domestic crisis with seriously adverse implications for American-Mexican relations.

In recent decades, America and Mexico have succeeded in constructing a predominantly positive relationship. However, their economic interdependence, their demographic interconnection due to years of high Mexican migration to the United States, and their shared security threat emanating from the cross-border narcotics trade makes relations between the two countries both more complex and also more vulnerable to the impact of international changes. Americans tend to take Mexico's relative stability for granted, assuming it poses little direct threat to America's strategic position and to the security of the entire Western Hemisphere. A significant deterioration in the US-Mexico relationship and its resulting consequences would thus come as a painful shock to the American public, generally not aware that the Mexican and American versions of their countries' past relations tend to vary.

Mexican-American relations have been historically both contentious and cooperative. Conflict has often occurred when Mexico was afflicted with internal violence and political turmoil, with America fearing a spillover into its territory but also exploiting the resulting opportunity to gain territory at the expense of its weaker neighbor. America's inconsistent and sometimes self-serving application of the Monroe Doctrine, its wars of expansion that resulted in it seizing Texas, California, and the American Southwest in 1848—then over 50% of Mexico's whole territory—and President Wilson's unpopular occupation of Veracruz during the Mexican Revolution provide the most prominent examples. On the other hand, cooperation between the two (as well as Canada) led to the creation of NAFTA, now the single largest economic zone in the world.

The two centuries of both worse and better Mexican-American relations are a reminder of the inherent difficulty of managing such an asymmetrical relationship. Domestic fears on both sides, political instability in Mexico, and the periodic assertiveness of US power often constricted what should have been a burgeoning partnership. Their close geographic proximity only compounded those issues, making economic and security cooperation more essential to national success but political instability and cultural fears more inhibiting to their neighborly cooperation. Thus, with intermittent periods of great compromise and acute tension, sustaining a constructive Mexican-American partnership has been a challenge to the leadership in both nations.

America and Mexico share cultural and personal links as well as economic and security concerns, all of which make a regional partnership mutually beneficial. America's economic resilience and political stability have so far also mitigated many of the challenges posed by such sensitive issues as economic dependence, immigration, and the narcotics trade. However, a decline in American power would likely undermine the health and good judgment of America's economic and political system, therefore intensifying the particular difficulties mentioned above. A waning United States would likely be more nationalistic, more defensive about its national identity, more paranoid about its homeland security, and less willing to sacrifice resources for the sake of others' development. Hence stable cooperation with Mexico would enjoy less popular support.

In such a setting, domestic politics in the United States would be likely to turn more protectionist, much like European powers did in the aftermath of World War I. The United States would be less likely to create institutions (such as the proposed North American Development Bank) to help foster regional—particularly Mexican—economic growth through jointly funded initiatives and more likely to impose subsidies to support powerful domestic constituencies to the detriment of Mexican exports. America's role as global leader has often helped protect American trade policy from the effects of protectionist-oriented domestic interests.

The resulting consequences would severely damage the Mexican economy, creating social and political aftershocks that would complicate further the next two most important issues in the Mexican-American relationship: immigration and the narcotics trade. Both issues are the target of tense, sometimes begrudging cooperation between America and Mexico. America's fair treatment of Mexican immigrants and its commitment to help Mexico combat the drug trade are essential to sustaining a productive partnership. However, the domestic and regional outlook of an America in decline would almost certainly increase American demonization of Mexican immigration and American skepticism regarding Mexico's will to combat its drug cartels. The United States would be likely to pursue more coercive solutions to these issues (i.e., cut off or deport immigrants, build up or deploy troops at the border), thus scuttling the good-neighbor policy and possibly igniting a geopolitical confrontation.

Mexican immigration, especially illegal immigration, is the result of the sharp contrast between economic and political conditions in Mexico and the United States. Over time, these differences have led to massive Mexican migration to America, such that the population of Mexican immigrants in America was estimated at around 11.5 million in 2009.[6] The estimated population of illegal Mexican immigrants in the United States is said to be 6.6 million.[7] And, the total population of individuals who are ethnically Mexican in America is now around 31 million or 10% of the total US population, most of whom remain deeply tied to their families in Mexico. Likewise, citizens of Mexico and the Mexican government itself are understandably concerned with the condition of immigrants in the United States. For example, Arizona's strict 2010 immigration law, aimed at increasing the prosecution and deportation of illegal immigrants, angered many in Mexico. Though President Obama denounced the bill, it still produced a sharp drop in the favorability with which Mexicans viewed Americans. According to the 2010 Pew Global Attitudes Survey, 44% of the Mexicans polled viewed the United States favorably after the enactment of the Arizona law, compared to 62% before.

A more coercive US attitude and policy toward Mexican immigrants would heighten Mexican resentment, adversely affecting the overall US-Mexico partnership. After 9/11, the issue of border security has come to be seen as essential to homeland security; the specter of an Islamic terrorist crossing the border from Mexico enhanced popular cries to seal off the border completely. America's decision to construct a wall/fence to separate itself from Mexico as a mechanism to support border security has already stimulated anti-American sentiments. It evokes negative images of Israel's construction of a "security barrier" in the West Bank or of the Berlin Wall. An internationally declining America is likely to become even more disturbed by the insecurity of its porous border with Mexico and the resulting immigration, inspiring a continuation of similar policies and creating a dangerous downward spiral for relations between the two neighbors.

Growing antagonism can also only further complicate both nations' ability to cooperate on the narcotics trade, an issue already of acute mutual concern. As a result of America's highly successful efforts to eliminate the Colombian drug trade, Mexico has increasingly inherited Colombia's role; 90% of all cocaine bound for the United States now goes through Mexico. This new reality has escalated violence in Mexico, for example in Juárez, and created spillover effects in the United States. And while America and Mexico have made combating the cross-border drug trade a policy priority, the problem has proven difficult to solve. The related violence has intensified and the corruption has persisted. It has been estimated that since 2006 about 5,000 Mexicans have died in drug-related violence, with 535 Mexican police officers perishing in 2009.[8]

In short, this has produced unsustainable pressure on Mexico's local and national governments and on law enforcement in the United States.

Defeating the narcotics pandemic would become exponentially more difficult if the United States declined, its financial and military resources dwindled, and its policies became more unilateral. Should the current strong north-south partnership then cease to exist because of growing anti-Americanism in Mexico resulting from America's economic protectionism and harsh immigration policies, the subsequent reorientation of the Mexican government away from full cooperation with the United States would weaken the effectiveness of any American counternarcotics efforts. Furthermore, a Mexican government lacking US support would find it impossible to defeat the drug cartels, and the political landscape in Mexico thus would become susceptible to political pressures for accommodation with drug lords at the expense of American security. This would return Mexico to levels of corruption equal to and beyond those present in Mexico prior to the shift of power from the Institutional Revolutionary Party (PRI) to an open, multiparty democracy in 2000. A return to such a state would stimulate further anti-Mexican tendencies in the United States.

A waning partnership between America and Mexico could precipitate regional and even international realignments. A reduction in Mexico's democratic values, its economic power, and its political stability coupled with the dangers of drug cartel expansion would limit Mexico's ability to become a regional leader with a proactive and positive agenda. This, in the end, could be the ultimate impact of an American decline: a weaker, less stable, less economically viable and more anti-American Mexico unable to constructively compete with Brazil for cooperative regional leadership or to help promote stability in Central America.

In that context, China could also begin to play a more significant role in the post-American regional politics of the Western Hemisphere. As part of China's slowly emerging campaign for greater global influence, the PRC has initiated large-scale investments in both Africa and Latin America. For example, Brazil and China have long been trying to forge a strategic partnership in energy and technology. This is not to suggest that China would seek to dominate this region, but it obviously could benefit from receding American regional power, by helping more overtly anti-American governments in their economic development.

In the longer run, the potential worsening of relations between a declining America and an internally troubled Mexico could even give rise to a particularly ominous phenomenon: the emergence, as a major issue in nationalistically aroused Mexican politics, of territorial claims justified by history and ignited by cross-border incidents. Political and economic realities have forced Mexicans to sublimate historical memories of territory lost to the United States for the sake of more beneficial relations with the most powerful state in the Western Hemisphere and (later) the sole global superpower. But in a world where Mexico did not count as much on a weakened United States, incidents resulting initially from the cross-border narcotics trade could easily escalate into armed clashes. One could even imagine cross-border raids made under the banner of "recovery" of historically Mexican soil; there are historical precedents for such a transformation of banditry into a patriotic cause. An additional and convenient pretext could be the notion that anti-immigrant sentiment in the United States is tantamount to discrimination, thus requiring retaliatory acts. These in turn could lead to the argument that the presence of many Mexicans on the formerly Mexican territory raises the issue of territorial self-determination.

Speculation along these lines reads today like futuristic fiction, unrelated to reality, but geopolitical realities would change dramatically in the event of America's decline. That could well include the once-hostile but lately amicable relationship between America and Mexico. And if that were to happen, America's geopolitically secure location free of neighborly conflicts, identified earlier in Part 2 as one of America's major assets, would become a thing of the past.

4: The Uncommon Global Commons

The global commons, those areas of the world that are shared by all states, can be reduced to two main sets of global concerns: the strategic and the environmental. The strategic commons include the sea and air, space, and cyberspace domains, as well as the nuclear domain as it pertains to controlling global proliferation. The environmental commons include the geopolitical implications of managing water sources, the Arctic, and global climate change. In these areas America, thanks to its near global hegemonic status, has had in recent years the opportunity to shape what has been called the "new world order." However, while American participation and, very often, American leadership have been essential to reforming and protecting the global commons, the United States has not always been on the front lines of progress. America, like any other great power, tried to construct a world that first and foremost benefited its own development even though during the twentieth century the United States at times was more idealistically motivated than previous dominant states in history.

Today the world's emerging powers—China, India, Brazil, and Russia—are playing a more integral role in this global management process. An American-European consensus or an American-Russian consensus alone cannot effectively dictate the rules of the commons. These new players are—though slowly—rising, necessitating a larger consensus group in securing and reforming the global commons. Nonetheless, American participation and co-leadership remains essential to solving new and old challenges.

The strategic commons will likely be the area most impacted by the shifting paradigm of global power, as relates to both the gradual growth in the capabilities and activism of emerging powers like China and India and the potential decline of American primacy. The sea and air, space, and cyberspace central to every country's national interest are dominated for the most part by America. In the coming years, however, they will become increasingly crowded and competitive as the power and national ambitions of other major states expand, and overall global power disperses.

Because control over the strategic commons is based on material advantages, as other nations grow their military capacities they will necessarily challenge the omnipresent position of the United States, in hopes to replace the United States as regional power broker. This competition could easily lead to miscalculation, less effective management, or a nationalistic territorial interstate rivalry in the strategic commons. China, for example, sees its surrounding waters as an extension of its territory. It considers most of the disputed islands there to be its own, and China has focused on developing naval capabilities aimed at denying America access to the South and East China Seas in order to protect those claims and solidify its regional position. Moreover, China has recently escalated disagreements over the limits of its territorial waters and over the ownership of the Senkaku, Paracel, and Spratly Islands into international disputes. Russia has also recently decided to make the navy its highest military priority, heavily increasing the funding for its Pacific Fleet. India too continues to expand its naval capabilities in the Indian Ocean.

The key to future stability in the strategic commons is to gradually develop a global consensus for an equitable and peaceful allocation of responsibilities while America's power is extant. For example, a peaceful maritime system is essential to the success of a globalized economy and all nations have an interest in seeing the air and seas managed in a responsible fashion because of their impact on international trade. Thus, a fair system for allocating management responsibilities is highly likely, even in the evolving landscape of regional power. However, in the short term, when such a system is only just emerging, one nation might well miscalculate its own power vis-à-vis its neighbor or seek to take an advantage at the expense of the greater community. This could result in significant conflicts, especially as nations press for greater access to energy resources beneath disputed waters.

America's decline would have dangerous implications for this strategic common since currently the world relies de facto on the United

States to manage and deter maritime conflicts. While it is unlikely that an American decline would severally inhibit its naval capacity—since it is central to America's core interests—a receding United States might be unable or simply reluctant to deter the escalation of maritime disputes in the Pacific or Indian Oceans, two areas of particular concern.

Similarly, outer space, an arena currently dominated by the United States, is beginning to experience greater activity thanks to the growing capabilities of emerging powers. The two most pressing issues regarding space are the increasing presence of space debris and space weaponry, both of which are being compounded by the surge in international space activity. When China successfully launched an antisatellite missile in 2007, destroying one of its own satellites, it added an unprecedented amount of dangerous debris to the low earth orbit and raised the level of uncertainty regarding China's intentions to militarize outer space.

While the United States has the most advanced tracking system of orbiting entities in the world and, therefore, possesses the ability to protect some of its assets, the rules regulating space activity need to be updated to reflect the post–Cold War environment, ensure the tranquility of space, and prohibit actions like that of China in 2007. But, if an American decline forces the United States to reduce its own space capabilities, or, much more likely, allows—in the midst of its decline—other emerging powers like China or India to consider space a viable domain in which to test their technology, herald their growing influence, and initiate a new strategic competition, the "final frontier" could become ominously unstable.

The Internet has become now what outer space used to be: the limitless frontier for commerce, communication, exploration, and power projection. Militaries, businesses, and government bureaucracies alike rely on a free and safe cyberspace for the successful execution of their responsibilities. However, maintaining the freedom of the Internet while simultaneously ensuring the security of information is a serious challenge, especially given the decentralized and rapidly evolving landscape of the Internet. American power in cyberspace, like in the oceans, has been essential to the fair regulation and freedom of the Internet because the United States currently controls—via a private nonprofit entity based out of California called the Internet Corporation for Assigned Names and Numbers (ICANN)—most of the access to and oversight of cyberspace. The world's resentment of American hegemonic control over the Internet coupled with the nuisance of cyber espionage and the serious threat of cyber warfare complicates the difficult task of managing this strategic common.

While this system allows the Internet to function, it does not prohibit individual nations, such as China or Iran, from limiting their own citizens' access to the Internet; although the United States has made it a priority to publicly oppose such restrictions. Thus, it is possible that in the absence of a strong America, emerging powers, particularly those nations not supportive of democracy or individual political rights, will exploit the lack of any political restraints and try to alter the working characteristics of the Internet, so as to more effectively restrict the Internet's potential beyond even their national boundaries.

In addition, the control of global nuclear proliferation is essential to the stability of the international system. For some years now, the United States has been the most vocal proponent of minimizing proliferation, even setting as its goal a world with zero nuclear weapons. Moreover, the United States provides security guarantees to specific non–nuclear weapon states that fear their nuclear neighbors by extending to them the US nuclear umbrella. Because the United States is the largest and most advanced nuclear weapon state and because its global position depends on the stability provided by its nuclear umbrella, the responsibility for leadership in the nuclear nonproliferation domain sits squarely on American shoulders. In this domain above all others the world still looks to the United States to lead.

Iran's pursuit of nuclear weapons today, combined with the possible American decline tomorrow, highlights the potential dangers of continuing nuclear proliferation in the twenty-first century: the fading of the nonproliferation regime, greater proliferation among emerging states, extensions of the Russian, Chinese, and Indian nuclear umbrellas, the intensifying of regional nuclear arms races, and the greater availability of nuclear material for theft by terrorist organizations.

An American decline would impact the nuclear domain most profoundly by inciting a crisis of confidence in the credibility of the American nuclear umbrella. Countries like South Korea, Taiwan, Japan, Turkey, and even Israel, among others, rely on the United States' extended nuclear deterrence for security. If they were to see the United States slowly retreat from certain regions, forced by circumstances to pull back its guarantees, or even if they were to lose confidence in standing US guarantees, because of the financial, political, military, and diplomatic consequences of an American decline, then they will have to seek security elsewhere. That "elsewhere" security could originate from only two sources: from nuclear weapons of one's own or from the extended deterrence of another power—most likely Russia, China, or India.

It is possible that countries that feel threatened by the ambition of existing nuclear weapon states, the addition of new nuclear weapon states, or the decline in the reliability of American power would develop their own nuclear capabilities. For crypto-nuclear powers like Germany and Japan, the path to nuclear weapons would be easy and fairly quick, given their extensive civilian nuclear industry, their financial success, and their technological acumen. Furthermore, the continued existence of nuclear weapons in North Korea and the potentiality of a nuclear-capable Iran could prompt American allies in the Persian Gulf or East Asia to build their own nuclear deterrents. Given North Korea's increasingly aggressive and erratic behavior, the failure of the six-party talks, and the widely held distrust of Iran's megalomaniacal leadership, the guarantees offered by a declining America's nuclear umbrella might not stave off a regional nuclear arms race among smaller powers.

Last but not least, even though China and India today maintain a responsible nuclear posture of minimal deterrence and "no first use," the uncertainty of an increasingly nuclear world could force both states to reevaluate and escalate their nuclear posture. Indeed, they as well as Russia might even become inclined to extend nuclear assurances to their respective client states. Not only could this signal a renewed regional nuclear arms race between these three aspiring powers but it could also create new and antagonistic spheres of influence in Eurasia driven by competitive nuclear deterrence.

The decline of the United States would thus precipitate drastic changes to the nuclear domain. An increase in proliferation among insecure American allies and/or an arms race between the emerging Asian powers are among the more likely outcomes. This ripple effect of proliferation would undermine the transparent management of the nuclear domain and increase the likelihood of interstate rivalry, miscalculation, and eventually even perhaps of international nuclear terror.

In addition to the foregoing, in the course of this century the world will face a series of novel geopolitical challenges brought about by significant changes in the physical environment. The management of those changing environmental commons—the growing scarcity of fresh water, the opening of the Arctic, and global warming—will require global consensus and mutual sacrifice. American leadership alone is not enough to secure cooperation on all these issues, but a decline in American influence would reduce the likelihood of achieving cooperative agreements on environmental and resource management. America's retirement from its role of global policeman could create greater opportunities for emerging powers to further exploit the environmental commons for their own economic gain, increasing the chances of resource-driven conflict, particularly in Asia.

The latter is likely to be the case especially in regard to the increasingly scarce water resources in many countries. According to the United States Agency for International Development (USAID), by 2025 more than 2.8 billion people will be living in either water-scarce or water-stressed regions, as global demand for water will double every twenty years.[9] While much of the Southern Hemisphere is threatened by potential water scarcity, interstate conflicts—the geopolitical consequences of cross-border water scarcity—are most likely to occur in Central and South Asia, the Middle East, and northeastern Africa, regions where limited water resources are shared across borders and political stability is transient. The combination of political insecurity and resource scarcity is a menacing geopolitical combination.

The threat of water conflicts is likely to intensify as the economic growth and increasing demand for water in emerging powers like Turkey and India collides with instability and resource scarcity in rival countries like Iraq and Pakistan. Water scarcity will also test China's internal stability as its burgeoning population and growing industrial complex combine to increase demand for and decrease supply of usable water. In South Asia, the never-ending political tension between India and Pakistan combined with overcrowding and Pakistan's heightening internal crises may put the Indus Water Treaty at risk, especially because the river basin originates in the long-disputed territory of Jammu and Kashmir, an area of ever-increasing political and military volatility. The lingering dispute between India and China over the status of Northeast India, an area through which the vital Brahmaputra River flows, also remains a serious concern. As American hegemony disappears and regional competition intensifies, disputes over natural resources like water have the potential to develop into full-scale conflicts.

The slow thawing of the Arctic will also change the face of the international competition for important resources. With the Arctic becoming increasingly accessible to human endeavor, the five Arctic littoral states—the United States, Canada, Russia, Denmark, and Norway—may rush to lay claim to its bounty of oil, gas, and metals. This run on the Arctic has the potential to cause severe shifts in the geopolitical landscape, particularly to Russia's advantage. As Vladimir Radyuhin points out in his article entitled "The Arctic's Strategic Value for Russia," Russia has the most to gain from access to the Arctic while simultaneously being the target of far north containment by the other four Arctic states, all of which are members of NATO. In many respects this new great game will be determined by who moves first with the most legitimacy, since very few agreements on the Arctic exist. The first Russian supertanker sailed from Europe to Asia via the North Sea in the summer of 2010.[10]

Russia has an immense amount of land and resource potential in the Arctic. Its territory within the Arctic Circle is 3.1 million square kilometers—around the size of India—and the Arctic accounts for 91% of Russia's natural gas production, 80% of its explored natural gas reserves, 90% of its offshore hydrocarbon reserves, and a large store of metals.[11] Russia is also attempting to increase its claim on the territory by asserting that its continental shelf continues deeper into the Arctic, which could qualify Russia for a 150-mile extension of its Exclusive Economic Zone and add another 1.2 million square kilometers of resource-rich territory. Its first attempt at this extension was denied by the UN Commission on the Continental Shelf, but it is planning to reapply in 2013. Russia considers the Arctic a true extension of its northern border and in a 2008 strategy paper President Medvedev stated that the Arctic would become Russia's "main strategic resource base" by 2020.[12]

Despite recent conciliatory summits between Europe and Russia over European security architecture, a large amount of uncertainty and distrust stains the West's relationship with Russia. The United States itself has always maintained a strong claim on the Arctic and has continued patrolling the area since the end of the Cold War. This was reinforced during the last month of President Bush's second term when he released a national security directive stipulating that America should "preserve the global mobility of the United States military and civilian vessels and aircraft throughout the Arctic region." The potentiality of an American decline could embolden Russia to more forcefully assert its control of the Arctic and over Europe via energy politics; though much depends on Russia's political orientation after the 2012 presidential elections. All five Arctic littoral states will benefit from a peaceful and cooperative agreement on the Arctic—similar to Norway's and Russia's 2010 agreement over the Barents Strait—and the geopolitical stability it would provide. Nevertheless, political circumstances could rapidly change in an environment where control over energy remains Russia's single greatest priority.

Global climate change is the final component of the environmental commons and the one with the greatest potential geopolitical impact. Scientists and policy makers alike have projected catastrophic consequences for mankind and the planet if the world average temperature rises by more than two degrees over the next century. Plant and animal species could grow extinct at a rapid pace, large-scale ecosystems could collapse, human migration could increase to untenable levels, and global economic development could be categorically reversed. Changes in geography, forced migration, and global economic contraction layered on top of the perennial regional security challenges could create a geopolitical reality of unmanageable complexity and conflict, especially in the densely populated and politically unstable areas of Asia such as the Northeast and South. Furthermore, any legitimate action inhibiting global climate change will require unprecedented levels of self-sacrifice and international cooperation. The United States does consider climate change a serious concern, but its lack of both long-term strategy and political commitment, evidenced in its refusal to ratify the Kyoto Protocol of 1997 and the repeated defeat of climate-change legislation in Congress, deters other countries from participating in a global agreement.

The United States is the second-largest global emitter of carbon dioxide, after China, with 20% of the world's share. The United States is the number one per capita emitter of carbon dioxide and the global leader in per capita energy demand. Therefore, US leadership is essential in not only getting other countries to cooperate, but also in actually inhibiting climate change. Others around the world, including the European Union and Brazil, have attempted their own domestic reforms on carbon emissions and energy use, and committed themselves to pursuing renewable energy. Even China has made reducing emissions a goal, a fact it refuses to let the United States ignore. But none of those nations currently has the ability to lead a global initiative. President Obama committed the United States to energy and carbon reform at the Copenhagen Summit in 2009, but the increasingly polarized domestic political environment and the truculent American economic recovery are unlikely to inspire progress on costly energy issues.

China is also critically important to any discussion of the management of climate change as it produces 21% of the world's total carbon emissions, a percentage that will only increase as China develops the western regions of its territory and as its citizens experience a growth in their standard of living. China, however, has refused to take on a leadership role in climate change, as it has also done in the maritime, space, and cyberspace domains. China uses its designation as a developing country to shield itself from the demands of global stewardship. China's tough stance at the 2009 Copenhagen Summit underscores the potential dangers of an American decline: no other country has the capacity and the desire to accept global stewardship over the environmental commons.

Only a vigorous Unites States could lead on climate change, given Russia's dependence on carbon-based energies for economic growth, India's relatively low emissions rate, and China's current reluctance to assume global responsibility. The protection and good faith management of the global commons—sea, space, cyberspace, nuclear proliferation, water security, the Arctic, and the environment itself—are imperative to the long-term growth of the global economy and the continuation of basic geopolitical stability. But in almost every case, the potential absence of constructive and influential US leadership would fatally undermine the essential communality of the global commons.

The argument that America's decline would generate global insecurity, endanger some vulnerable states, produce a more troubled North American neighborhood, and make cooperative management of the global commons more difficult is not an argument for US global supremacy. In fact, the strategic complexities of the world in the twenty-first century—resulting from the rise of a politically self-assertive global population and from the dispersal of global power—make such supremacy unattainable. But in this increasingly complicated geopolitical environment, an America in pursuit of a new, timely strategic vision is crucial to helping the world avoid a dangerous slide into international turmoil.

- PART 4 -

Beyond 2025: A New Geopolitical Balance

AMERICA'S GLOBAL STANDING IN THE DECADES AHEAD WILL DEPEND on its successful implementation of purposeful efforts to overcome its drift toward a socioeconomic obsolescence and to shape a new and stable geopolitical equilibrium on the world's most important continent by far, Eurasia.

The key to America's future is thus in the hands of the American people. America can significantly upgrade its domestic condition and redefine its central international role in keeping with the new objective and subjective conditions of the twenty-first century. In order to achieve this, it is essential that America undertake a national effort to enhance the public's understanding of America's changing, and potentially dangerous, global circumstances. America's inherent assets, as discussed previously, still justify cautious optimism that such a renewal can refute the prognoses of America's irreversible decline and global irrelevance, but public ignorance of the growing overall vulnerability of America's domestic and foreign standing must be tackled deliberately, head-on, and from the top down.

Democracy is simultaneously one of America's greatest strengths and one of the central sources of its current predicament. America's founders designed its constitutional system so that most decisions could only be made incrementally. Therefore, truly comprehensive national decisions require a unique degree of consensus, generated by dramatic and socially compelling circumstances (such as, at their extreme, a great financial crisis or an imminent external threat) and/or propelled by the persuasive impact of determined national leadership. And since in America only the President has a voice that resonates nationally, the President must drive America's renewal forward.

As both candidate and President, Barack Obama has delivered several remarkable speeches. He has spoken directly and in a historically sensitive manner to Europeans, Middle Easterners, Muslims, and Asians, addressing the necessarily changing relationship of America to their concerns. In particular, President Obama's speeches in Prague and Cairo raised the world's expectations regarding the orientation of America's future foreign policy. International public opinion polls showed an almost immediate and positive reaction in the world's perception of America as a whole because of President Obama's image and rhetoric. Yet he has failed to speak directly to the American people about America's changing role in the world, its implications, and its demands.

The tragedy of September 11, 2001, fundamentally altered America's own view of its global purpose. Building off of the public's basic ignorance of world history and geography, profit-motivated mass media exploited public fears allowing for the demagogically inclined Bush administration to spend eight years remaking the United States into a crusader state. The "war on terror" became synonymous with foreign policy and the United States, for the most part, neglected to build a strategy that addressed its long-term interests in an evolving geopolitical environment. Thus, America was left unprepared—thanks to the confluence of the above—to face the novel challenges of the twenty-first century.

America and its leaders need to understand the new strategic landscape so that they can embrace a domestic and foreign renewal aimed at revitalizing America's global role. What follows addresses the demands of the evolving geopolitical conditions and provides, in response, the outline of a timely vision for US foreign policy.

1: Eurasia's Geopolitical Volatility

Both the most immediate foreign policy threat to America's global status and the longer-range challenge to global geopolitical stability arise on the Eurasian continent. The immediate threat is currently located in the region east of Egypt's Suez Canal, west of China's Xinjiang Province, south of Russia's post-Soviet frontiers in the Caucasus and with the new central Asian states. The longer-range challenge to global stability arises out of the still-continuing and consequentially unpredictable shift in the global center of gravity from the West to the East (or from Europe to Asia and perhaps even from America to China).

America, more than any other power, has become directly involved in a series of conflicts within Eurasia. It is a telling fact that regional powers potentially more directly affected by the consequences of what happens in that volatile area—such as India, Russia, and China—have stayed carefully away from any direct participation in America's painful (at times, inept) efforts to cope with the region's slide into escalating ethnic and religious conflict.

Ultimately, any constructive solution to the Afghan conflict has to combine an internal political accommodation between the government in Kabul and rival Afghan factions within an external regional framework in which Afghanistan's principal neighbors assume a major role in contributing to the country's stability. As argued earlier, protracted and largely American military involvement is neither the solution to the Afghan tragedy initiated by the Soviet invasion of the country nor is it likely to provide regional stability. Similarly, the regional challenge posed by Iran can be resolved neither by an Israeli nor by an American military strike against Iranian nuclear facilities now under construction. Such actions would simply fuse Iranian nationalism with belligerent fundamentalism, producing a protracted conflict with highly destabilizing consequences for the few still pro-Western Arab regimes of the Middle East. In the long run, Iran also has to be assimilated into a process of regional accommodation.

In any case, America can still contain a nuclear Iran. In the past, America had successfully deterred the use of nuclear weapons by the Soviet Union and China—despite at times extreme belligerence by both countries—and eventually produced conditions favorable to an American-Russian as well as an American-Chinese accommodation. America, moreover, has the capacity to provide an effective nuclear shield for all of the Middle East in the event that it becomes evident that Iran is actually acquiring nuclear weapons. Hence, if Iran does not reach an acceptable accommodation with the world community, providing credible assurances that its nuclear program does not contain a secret nuclear weapons component, the United States should make a public commitment to consider any Iranian attempt at intimidating or threatening its Middle Eastern neighbors as a threat against the United States.

In that context, if it becomes clear that Iran is actually in the process of acquiring nuclear weapons, America could also seek commitments from other nuclear powers to participate in the collective enforcement of a UN resolution to disarm Iran, by compulsion if necessary. But it must be stressed: such enforcement would have to be collective and involve also Russia and China. America can provide a nuclear umbrella for the region by itself, but it should not engage in a solitary military action against Iran or just in cooperation with Israel, for that would plunge America into a wider, again lonely, and eventually self-destructive conflict.

Of equal importance to the problems of Afghanistan and Iran is America's stake in a constructive resolution of the Israeli-Palestinian conflict. This conflict poisons the atmosphere of the Middle East, contributes to Muslim extremism, and is directly damaging to American national interests. A positive outcome would greatly contribute to stability in the Middle East. Otherwise, American interests in the region will suffer, and eventually Israel's fate in such a hostile international environment will be in doubt.

These three interrelated issues are the most urgent items on America's current geopolitical agenda because of the immediacy of their potential impact. But the far-reaching changes in the distribution of global power signal the historic need—the foregoing crises aside—for the United States also to pursue a longer-term strategic vision of more stable and cooperative Eurasian geopolitics. At this stage, only America is in the position to promote the needed transcontinental equilibrium without which the percolating conflicts on this huge and now politically activated continent will dangerously escalate. Europe, alas, is looking inward, Russia still at its recent past, China to its own future, and India enviously at China.

Such a longer-term geostrategic effort has to focus on Eurasia as a whole. Its combination of competitive geopolitical motivations, political might, and economic dynamism make that huge trans-Eurasian continent the central arena of world affairs.* America—after its emergence in 1991 as the world's only superpower—had a unique opportunity to play an active role in helping to develop Eurasia's new international architecture in order to fill the void created by the disappearance of the once continentally dominant Sino-Soviet bloc. That opportunity was wasted, and so now the task has to be undertaken in circumstances considerably more challenging for America.

Eurasia, in the two decades since the end of the Cold War, has drifted. Europe has become less, not more, politically united, while in the meantime Turkey and Russia have both remained on the uncertain periphery of the Western community. In the East, China has grown in

---

* Its description in *The Grand Chessboard* (1997), p. 31, is still largely valid: "Eurasia is the globe's largest continent and is geopolitically axial. A power that dominates Eurasia would control two of the world's three most advanced and economically productive regions. A mere glance at the map also suggests that control over Eurasia would almost automatically entail Africa's subordination. . . . About 75% of the world's people live in Eurasia, and most of the world's physical wealth is there as well, both in its enterprises and underneath its soil. . . . After the United States, the next six largest economies and the next six biggest spenders on military weaponry are located in Eurasia. All but one of the world's overt nuclear powers and all but one of the covert ones are located in Eurasia. The world's two most populist aspirants to regional hegemony and global influence are Eurasian."

economic, political, and military might, creating anxiety in a region already beset with historic rivalries. America must fashion a policy relevant to the challenges on both sides of Eurasia in order to ensure the stability of the continent as a whole.

In the West, the European Union failed to use the years of "Europe whole and free" to make Europe truly whole and its freedom firmly secure. A monetary union is not a substitute for real political unity, not to mention that a monetary union based on very unequal national resources and obligations could not foster a binding sense of transnational unity. Concurrent economic tribulations, which magnified after 2007 particularly in southern Europe, made the notion of Europe as a political and military heavyweight increasingly illusory. Europe, once the center of the West, became an extension of a West whose defining player is America.

However, the unity of that currently America-dominated West should not be taken for granted. Not only do the members of the EU lack a genuinely shared transnational political identity—not to mention a common global role—but also they are potentially vulnerable to deepening geostrategic cleavages. Great Britain clings to its special attachment to the United States and to a special status in the EU. France, envious of Germany's rising stature as the prime power of the EU, keeps seeking a preeminent role for itself by periodic overtures for shared leadership with America, Russia, or Germany, not to mention leadership of the amorphous Mediterranean Union. Germany increasingly toys with Bismarckian notions of a special relationship with Russia, which inevitably frightens some Central Europeans into pleading for ever-closer security links with the United States.

All European countries, moreover, are opting out of any serious commitment to their own, or even to NATO-based, collective security. In different ways, its rapidly aging population as well as its youth care far more for their social security than for their national security. Basically, the United States is increasingly left with the ultimate responsibility for Europe's security, in the reassuring hope that America will remain committed to preserving the frontiers of "Europe whole and free." But these boundaries could be leapfrogged by the emerging German-Russian special relationship, driven on Germany's side by the irresistible attraction to its business elite (as well as to the Italian and some others) of the commercial prospects of a modernizing Russia. The European Union thus faces the prospect of deepening geostrategic divisions, with some key states tempted by the option of a privileged business as well as political relationship with Russia.

The foregoing is particularly a cause both for regret and concern because the European enterprise holds great and already demonstrated potential for the democratic and social transformation of the European east. The enlargement of the EU to Central Europe (which during the Cold War was usually referred to as Eastern Europe) has already generated far-reaching institutional and infrastructural reforms in the region, most significantly in Poland, providing an example that is becoming increasingly attractive to the peoples of the adjoining Ukraine and Belarus. In time, Europe's example could become a truly compelling transformative influence on both Turkey and Russia, especially if a geopolitically more active Europe, together with America, were guided by a shared long-term goal to engage them in a larger and more vital Western community.

That requires, however, a long-term vision and an equally long-term strategy for executing it. But today's Europe—along with America—lacks both. It is ironic that even in the geographically distant Korea the country's leading newspaper published in the fall of 2010 an apt indictment of Europe's strategic self-indulgence, bluntly stating that:

> It would be wrong, of course, to suggest that Europe has suddenly become a political backwater. But it is true that Europeans need to take a long, hard look at themselves and at where they will be in 40 years if current trends continue. What is needed today is a clear definition of Europe's interests—and its responsibilities. Europe needs a sense of purpose for a

> century in which many of the odds will be stacked against it, as well as a statement of the moral standards that will guide its actions and, one hopes, its leadership.[1]

So, the question "where Europe will be forty years from now?" is directly germane in geopolitical terms to the future of Europe's relationship with its geographic east, and that should be of equal concern both to Europe and to America. What should be the eastern boundary of a larger Europe and thus of the West? What roles could Turkey and Russia play were they truly to become part of a larger West? Conversely, what would be the consequences for Europe and America were Turkey and Russia to remain—in part because of European prejudice and American passivity—outside of Europe and thus also outside of the West?

In Turkey, its ongoing but unfinished transformation has in fact been modeled from its very start on Europe, with the announcement in 1921 by Ataturk (Mustafa Kemal), the leader of the "Young Turks" movement, of the decision to transform the Turkish ethnic core of the fallen and dismembered Ottoman Empire into a modern European-type secular nation-state, to be known henceforth as Turkey. In more recent times, its modernization evolved into democratization, a process to a significant degree driven by Turkey's interest in becoming more explicitly a part of the unifying Europe. The Turkish aspiration was encouraged as early as the 1960s by the Europeans themselves, and it resulted in Turkey's official application for membership in 1987. In turn, that action led to the EU's decision in 2005 to start formal negotiations. And despite the recent hesitations of some members of the EU—particularly France and Germany—regarding Turkish membership, it is a geopolitical reality that a genuinely Western-type Turkish democracy, if solidly anchored in the West through more than just NATO, could be Europe's shield protecting it from the restless Middle East.

The case regarding Russia is more problematical in the short run, but in the longer term the pursuit of a similarly positive and far-reaching strategic engagement is becoming historically timely. Admittedly, Russia, twenty years after the fall of the Soviet Union, still remains undecided about its identity, nostalgic about its past, and simultaneously overreaching in some of its aspirations. Its efforts to create "a common economic space" (under the aegis of the Kremlin) in the area of the former Soviet Union naturally worry the newly independent post-Soviet states. The dominant elements in its power elite still maneuver to dilute transatlantic links, and they still resent Central Europe's desire for deep integration within the European Union and its defensive membership in NATO, even while also worrying about China's growing power on the very edge of Russia's mineral-rich and sparsely populated Far East.

At the same time, however, the increasingly politically important Russian middle class is evidently adopting the life-styles of the West while a growing number of Russia's intellectual community speak more openly of their desire for Russia to be a part of the modern West. The fundamental question "what is the right relationship between modernization and democratization?" has started to permeate informal debates within the country's upper strata, including even some segments of the top political elite entrenched in the Kremlin. A growing number of Russians are beginning to realize that a fundamental change in Russia's relationship with the West may be in the country's vital long-range interest.

Simultaneously, uncertainty regarding Asia's geopolitical stability is rising in the eastern half of Eurasia. Unless deliberately constrained, the competitive geopolitics of the newly energized Asia could become ominously reminiscent of conflicts in the West over the last two hundred years. China's ambitions are beginning to surface more openly, with nationalistic assertiveness increasingly undermining the carefully cultivated veil of official modesty, national moderation, and historic patience. Its competition for regional preeminence with Japan and with India is still primarily in the diplomatic and economic realms, but the availability of effective military power—and perhaps the willingness to use it—is becoming a relevant consideration in respective geopolitical calculations. Any use of force could become especially ominous in the rivalry between the nuclear-armed China and India, especially over the also nuclear-armed Pakistan. The rising new East could then, indeed, become quite turbulent, just as the old West once was.

As noted earlier, the southwest region of the awakened eastern part of Eurasia is already in a potentially contagious crisis. The new "Global Balkans"[2] embracing the Middle East, Iran, Afghanistan, and Pakistan—where the United States is the only major external power to have become militarily involved—risks expanding to Central Asia, with violence already intensifying in parts of Russia's Muslim-inhabited North Caucasus. Every one of the new Central Asian states is potentially vulnerable to internal violence, each of them is insecure, and all of them desire more direct access to the outside world while seeking to avoid either Russian or Chinese domination. The now politically awakened Eurasia as a whole thus lacks a shared framework and its geopolitical stability is questionable.

Over one hundred years ago the path-breaking geopolitical thinker, Harold Mackinder, identified Eurasia as the key "world-island" and concluded that "who rules the world-island, commands the world." In all of world history, only three ruthless heads of powerful military machines came even close to achieving such "rule." Genghis Khan almost did so by relying on his remarkable military skills, but his conquest of the "world-island" ended on the edge of Central Europe. He could not overcome the consequences of distance and of numbers, and consequently the numerically thin Mongol veneer of his "empire" was assimilated before long into the initially conquered populations.

Hitler, having conquered Europe, also came close to achieving from the opposite direction a similar outcome, and might have won if the Nazi invasion of Russia had been accompanied by a Japanese attack on Russia from the East. Then, after Hitler's defeat, with Soviet forces entrenched west of Berlin in the center of Europe, Stalin actually came the closest when his trans-Eurasian Sino-Soviet bloc, which emerged as a result of Communist victory in China, attempted to drive America out of Korea. However, the possibility of Communist control over the "world-island" faded rapidly as NATO was organized in the West and as the Sino-Soviet bloc in the East split after Stalin's death in a bitter and divisive feud.

Given the rise of the newly dynamic but also internationally complex and politically awakened Asia, the new reality is that no one power can any longer seek—in Mackinder's words—to "rule" Eurasia and thus to "command" the world. America's role, especially after having wasted twenty years, now has to be both subtler and more responsive to Eurasia's new realities of power. Domination by a single state, no matter how powerful, is no longer possible, especially given the emergence of new regional players. Accordingly, the timely and needed objective of a deliberate longer-term effort by America should be broad geopolitical trans-Eurasian stability based on increasing accommodation among the old powers of the West and the new powers of the East.

In essence, the pursuit of the foregoing objective will require US engagement in shaping a more vital and larger West while helping to balance the emerging rivalry in the rising and restless East. This complex undertaking will call for a sustained effort over the next several decades to connect, in transformative ways, through institutions like the EU and NATO, both Russia and Turkey with a West that already embraces both the EU and the United States. Steady but genuine progress along that axis could infuse a sense of strategic purpose into a Europe increasingly threatened by a slide into destabilizing and divisive geopolitical irrelevance. At the same time, America's strategic engagement in Asia should entail a carefully calibrated effort to nurture a cooperative partnership with China while deliberately promoting reconciliation between China and US-allied Japan, in addition to expanding friendly relations with such key states as India and Indonesia. Otherwise, Asian rivalries in general or fear of a dominant China in particular could undermine both Asia's new potential world role and its regional stability. The task ahead is to translate a long-term geopolitical vision into a historically sound and politically attractive strategy that promotes realistically the revival of the West and facilitates the stabilization of the East within a wider cooperative framework.

2: A Larger and Vital West

The earlier discussions of "The Receding West" and of "The Waning of the American Dream" were not exercises in historical inevitability. A renewal of American domestic dynamism is possible, while America, by working purposefully with Europe, can shape a larger and more vital West. The point of departure for such a long-term effort is recognition of the historical reality that the Europe of today is still unfinished business. And it will remain so until the West in a strategically sober and prudent fashion embraces Turkey on more equal terms and engages Russia politically as well as economically. Such an expanded West can help anchor the stability of an evolving Eurasia, as well as revitalize its own historic legacy.

The dividing line between Europe on the one hand and Russia and Turkey on the other is a geographical abstraction. Neither the rivers Bug (separating Poland from Belarus) nor Prut (separating Romania from Ukraine) nor Narva (separating Estonia from Russia) define the natural geographic and cultural outer limits of Europe's East. Nor, for that matter, do the Ural Mountains located deep within Russia, customarily cited in geography books as delineating Europe from Asia. Even less meaningful in that regard is the Strait of Bosporus, which links the Mediterranean and Black Seas, with the Turkish metropolis Istanbul said to be located in "Europe" but with the city's extension across the narrow passage of seawater (as well as the main part of Turkey's territory) said to be in "Asia."*

* Philip Johan van Strahlberg, a Swedish geographer who traveled throughout Russia in the early 1700s, popularized this idea of a geographic boundary between Europe and Asia through his book *An Historico-Geographical Description of the North and Eastern Parts of Europe and Asia* (London: W. Innys and R. Manby, 1738).

More misleading still are the conventional notions of the cultural boundaries of Europe. In terms of lifestyle, architecture, and social habits, Vladivostok in Russia's far east is more European than Kazan (the capital of Tatarstan) located thousands of miles west of Vladivostok in the "European" part of the Russian Federation. Ankara, the capital of Turkey located on the Anatolian Plain and thus geographically in Asia, is as thoroughly a European city as Yerevan, the capital of Armenia, located more than half a thousand miles further east but said to be in Europe.

Ultimately, contemporary Russia and, to a lesser degree, Turkey are separated from Europe neither by geography nor by lifestyle but rather by an ambivalence—difficult to define precisely—regarding what is politically and culturally distinctive to the current postimperial West: its shared combination of residual spiritual beliefs and philosophical principles, especially in regard to the sanctity of the individual, combined with widely accepted notions of civil rights enshrined in an explicit commitment to the rule of law in constitutionally defined democratic states. The Russians profess to share these values but their political system does not reflect them. The Turks for the most part already practice them, and both assert categorically that they already are "European" culturally and socially. Each minimizes the residual impact of their once more distinctive oriental despotisms. The Turks point to the institutionalized separation of religion and state in their own modernized and increasingly democratic Turkey. The Russians stress that as far back as under Peter the Great Russia was deliberately Europeanizing itself, that the recent Communist era was essentially an aberration, and that their Russian Orthodox traditions are an integral part of European Christendom.

Nonetheless, it is true that both Russia and Turkey are inheritors, though in different ways, of culturally distinctive imperial pasts that continue to blend with their contemporary "Europeanism." Both countries attained greatness apart from, and often against, Europe. And both subsequently experienced a deep fall. During the nineteenth century, Turkey was labeled "the sick man of Europe." In the course of the twentieth century, Russia was seen as such twice, first before the Bolshevik Revolution and then after the fall of Soviet Communism. Both have repudiated their respective imperial pasts but they cannot entirely erase them from either their geopolitical ambitions or from their historical consciousness as they deliberately and insistently redefine themselves.

During the twentieth century, Turkey proved more successful in transforming itself than Communist Russia. Ataturk's sweeping reforms, which were abruptly imposed on Turkey in 1924 (three years after its proclamation as a postimperial state), produced dramatic and remarkably successful changes. The country broke with its Arab-Islamic connection, it suddenly (literally overnight) adopted the Western alphabet in place of the Arabic script, it removed religious elements from its state institutions, and it even changed the people's dress code. In subsequent decades, it has progressively institutionalized in a determined fashion an increasingly democratic process within a firmly defined secular state.

Unlike Russia, at no time did Turkey either plunge into a Manichean orgy of internal killing or degenerate into totalitarianism. The ambitious nationalist mystique of Ataturk was contagious among fervent younger Turks, but it was not imposed by sustained, brutalizing, and lethal terror. There was no Gulag; nor was there any claim that what the Turks were doing domestically was universally applicable and historically inevitable. The Turkish experiment, in effect, was less globally ambitious than the Soviet but more nationally successful.

It is noteworthy that Turkey managed in an impressive fashion to shed its imperial ambitions and to redirect its national energy toward internal social modernization. In firmly promoting it, Ataturk was guided by a historic vision in which means were in balance with ends, thus avoiding the Stalinist excesses of Leninist utopianism and universalism. His vision also facilitated Turkey's remarkably realistic accommodation to its new postimperial status, especially in contrast to the still-lingering nostalgia among some portions of the Russian elite for its recently lost multinational empire.

In the course of the last two decades, Turkey has moved steadily forward in its consolidation of a genuinely functioning constitutional democracy, driven by its desire to join the EU—having been invited several decades ago to do so by the Europeans, but on the specific condition that Turkey would satisfy Europe's democratic standards. More importantly, however, Turkey's steady democratization has been a reflection of its growing acceptance of democracy as a way of life. Though its democracy is still vulnerable, especially in the area of press freedom, the fact that the Turkish military has had to acquiesce to electoral outcomes and constitutional changes it did not like is a testimonial to the vitality of Turkey's ongoing democracy. In that respect, Turkey is also clearly ahead of Russia.

Continued secularization will be critical to Turkey's democratic progress. Because Ataturk imposed secularization from above in 1924, many Europeans and even some Turks now fear that with the onset and subsequent acceleration in recent decades of Turkey's democratization, greater political openness could lead to the resurgence of more extreme manifestations of religious primacy in social affairs and even to the primacy of religious identity over national identity. That, so far at least, has not happened and some indications suggest that a more robust Turkish democracy gradually reduces the appeal of religious fundamentalism. For example, according to a Turkish university survey, between 1999 and 2009, public support for the adoption of sharia laws declined from over 25% to about 10%. Closer ties with Europe would be likely to favor the further social acceptance of a secular and national Turkish state.

It is also important to recognize that Turkey is already broadly connected in important ways to the West in general and to Europe specifically. It has been a stalwart member of NATO since its inception, more willing to help the Alliance in actual combat than some other European allies, and it has the second-largest standing armed force in NATO. It also maintained comprehensive and sensitive security links with the United States throughout the Cold War. For years it has been engaged in the tedious but necessary process of making its domestic law and constitutional practices compatible with EU standards. Thus de facto, though not yet as a legal fact, Turkey is in some significant ways already an informal extension of Europe and thus also of the West.

On the international arena, the increasingly modern and basically secular Turkey of today is beginning to attain a regional preeminence geographically derived from its imperial Ottoman past. Turkey's new foreign policy, shaped by its geopolitically minded Foreign Minister (Ahmet Davutoglu, the author of the concept of "Strategic Depth"), is premised on the notion that Turkey is a regional leader in the areas once part of the Ottoman Empire, including the Levant, North Africa, and Mesopotamia. This approach is not driven by religious considerations but has a historical-geopolitical motivation. Based on the reasonable premise that good relations with neighbors are preferable to hostile ones, Davutoglu's plan posits that Turkey should exploit its current socioeconomic dynamism—in 2010 it ranked as the world's seventeenth-largest economy—to rebuild relationships that existed historically but faded during the twentieth century because of Kemalist concentration on internal secularization and inculcation of a specifically Turkish nationalism.

Moreover, in the wake of the Soviet Union's dissolution and beyond the boundaries of the former Ottoman Empire, the newly independent Central Asia, largely Turkic in its cultural heritage, now beckons. Turkey's more active commercial and cultural outreach is a potential reinforcement for the modernization, secularization, and eventual democratization of this energy-rich but geopolitically inchoate region. It is also relevant to note that since Russia seeks to monopolize direct foreign access to Central Asian energy exports, Turkey's increasing regional role can facilitate—in joint collaboration with Azerbaijan and Georgia—Europe's unimpeded access across the Caspian Sea to Central Asia's oil and gas.

Turkey's increasingly promising transformation into a modern and secular state—in spite of some persisting retardation in some social aspects including press freedom, education, and human development (see comparative Turkey-Russia tables on p. 142–143)—invests its citizens with a patriotic self-confidence that could turn into enduring anti-Western animus if Turkey were to feel itself permanently rejected by Europe. Forces within Europe—predominately in France and Germany—continue to deny Turkish aspirations because of an ambiguous belief that Turkey is an alien culture that represents an intrusion rather than a partnership. Thus, eighty-five years after the initiation of their unprecedented effort at social modernization and cultural transformation based on the European example, the Turks are now becoming resentful of their continuing exclusion. And that contributes to the risk that if the democratic experiment in Turkey were to fail, Turkey could turn back toward a more assertive Islamic political identity or succumb to some form of nondemocratic military regimentation. In either case, Turkey, instead of shielding Europe from the problems and passions of the Middle East, would amplify those challenges through the Balkans into Europe.

That eventuality could become especially threatening in the event of a continued failure by America and Europe to achieve an Israeli-Palestinian peace of genuine accommodation, and/or if America plunges into a direct conflict with Iran. The former—resulting very likely in intensified extremism in the Middle East—would indirectly but still quite adversely influence Turkish attitudes toward the West; the latter would threaten Turkish security, especially if the conflict were to ignite a wider Kurdish insurgency and again destabilize Iraq. The Turks would resent the fact that their national interests were not only being ignored but also jeopardized by the West.

A prolonged separation from Europe morphing into hostility could generate a political retrogression and a fundamentalist revival that could then halt Turkey's march to modernity. In a worst-case scenario, reminiscent of the consequences for Iran of the Shah's overthrow in 1978, such separation could even undermine Ataturk's remarkable legacy. That would be historically and geopolitically unfortunate for three fundamental reasons. First, Turkey's internal democratization and spreading modernization is evidence that neither democratization nor modernization are incompatible with Islamic religious traditions. Such a demonstration is of great importance to the political future of the Islamic world as well as to global stability. Second, Turkey's commitment to peaceful cooperation with its Middle Eastern neighbors, a region of Turkey's historic preeminence, is consistent with the security interests of the West in that region. Third, a Turkey that is increasingly Western, secular, and yet also Islamic—and that exploits its territorial and cultural connection with the peoples of the old Ottoman Empire and the post-Soviet Central Asian states—could be a Turkey that undermines the appeal of Islamic extremism and enhances regional stability in Central Asia not only to its own benefit but also to that of Europe and Russia.

In contrast to Turkey, Russia's relationship with Europe is ambivalent. Its political elite proclaims that it desires closer links with the EU and NATO, but it is unwilling at this stage to adopt the reforms that would facilitate such linkage. Its social, political, and economic programs lack focus and their prospects remain relatively uncertain. Nevertheless, it is essential, for America, Europe, and Russia, that Russia forges a partnership with the West rooted in a commitment to shared political as well as economic values. The next two decades are likely to be critical for Russia in determining its prospects for greater—and politically genuine—collaboration with the West.

Historically, Russia considers itself to be too powerful to be satisfied with being merely a normal European state and yet has been too weak to permanently dominate Europe. It is noteworthy in this connection that its greatest military triumphs—notably, Alexander's victorious entry into Paris in 1815 and Stalin's celebratory dinner in Potsdam in mid-1945—were more the byproducts of the folly of Russia's enemies than the consequence of enduringly successful Russian statesmanship. Had Napoleon not attacked Russia in 1812, it is doubtful that Russian troops would have marched into Paris in 1815. For within less than five decades of Alexander's triumph, Russia was defeated in the Crimean War by an Anglo-French expeditionary force deployed from afar by sea. Five decades later in 1905, it was crushed in the Far East by the Japanese army and navy. In World War I, Russia was decisively defeated by a Germany that was fighting a prolonged two-front war. Stalin's victory in the middle of the twentieth century, precipitated by Hitler's folly, gained Russia political control over Eastern Europe and extended into the very heart of Europe. But within five decades of that triumph both the Soviet-controlled bloc of Communist states as well as the historic Russian empire itself disintegrated due to exhaustion resulting from the Cold War with America.

Nonetheless, the contemporary postimperial Russia—because of the wealth of its sparsely populated but vast territory rich in natural resources—is destined to play a significant role on the world arena. Yet historically, as a major international player, Russia has not displayed the diplomatic finesse of Great Britain, or the commercial acumen of the democratically appealing America, or the patient self-control of the historically self-confident China. It has failed to pursue consistently a state policy that prudently exploits its natural resources, extraordinary space, and impressive social talent to rise steadily while setting an international example of successful social development. Rather, Russia has tended to engage in bursts of triumphant and rather messianic self-assertion followed by plunges into lethargic morass.

Moreover, though Russia's territorial size automatically defines it as a great power, the socioeconomic condition of its people is detrimental to Russia's global standing. Widespread global awareness of Russia's social liabilities and relatively modest standard of living discredits its international aspirations. Its grave demographic crisis—a negative population growth marked by high death rates—is a testimonial to social failure, with the relatively short life span of its males being the consequence of widespread alcoholism and its resulting demoralization. At the same time, the growing uncertainties regarding rising Islamic unrest along its new southern borders and Russia's barely hidden anxieties regarding its increasingly powerful and densely populated Chinese neighbor, situated next to Russia's empty east, collide with Moscow's great power hubris.

In comparison to Turkey, Russia's social performance ratings—despite the fact that it ranks overall number one in territory, number nine in population, and number two in the number of its nuclear weapons—are actually somewhat worse and can be considered at best only middling in a worldwide comparison. In the area of longevity and population growth, Russia's numbers are disturbingly low. Cumulatively, Russia's and Turkey's ratings dramatize the dialectical reality that both are simultaneously in some respects advanced industrial countries and yet still somewhat underdeveloped societies, with Russia specifically handicapped by its nondemocratic and corruption-ridden political system. The comparisons with other countries ranked immediately above or below Turkey and Russia respectively are especially telling. Russia's demographic crisis, political corruption, outdated and resource-driven economic model, and social retardation pose especially serious obstacles to a genuine fulfillment of the understandable ambitions of its talented but often misruled people. The following tables (see Figure 4.1 on pp. 142–143) reinforce the proposition that both nations would benefit greatly from a genuinely transformative relationship with a Europe that is able to reach out confidently to the East because of its ongoing links to America.

Moreover, the persisting disregard specifically in Russia for the rule of law is perhaps its greatest impediment to a philosophical embrace with the West. Without an institutionalized supremacy of law, the adoption of a Western-type democracy in Russia has so far been no more than a superficial imitation. That reality encourages and perpetuates corruption as well as the abuse of civil rights, a tradition deeply embedded in the historically prolonged subordination of Russian society to the state.

Complicating matters further, the current geopolitical orientation of Russia's foreign policy elite, unlike Turkey's, is quite conflicted and in some respects escapist. At this time—and also in contrast to Turkey—full-fledged membership in the Atlantic community through eventual membership in its economic as well as political and security institutions is not yet Russia's explicit and dominant aspiration. In fact, there exist within Russia's political and business elites multiple interpretations of Russia's appropriate global role. Many wealthy Russian businessmen (especially in St. Petersburg and Moscow) would like Russia to be a modern, European-type society because of the resulting economic advantages. Meanwhile, many in the political elite desire Russia to be the dominant European power in a Europe detached from America, or even to be a world power on par with America. And still other Russians toy with the seemingly captivating notions of "Eurasianism," of Slavic Union, or even of an anti-Western alliance with the Chinese.

The "Eurasianists," mesmerized by the sheer geographic size of Russia, see it as a mighty Eurasian power, neither strictly European nor Asian, and destined to play a coequal role with America and China. They fail to realize that with their trans-Eurasian space largely empty and still underdeveloped, such a strategy is an illusion. A variant of this notion, the idea of a Russo-Chinese alliance presumably directed against America, also represents an escape from reality. The fact of the matter, painful for many Russians to acknowledge, is that in such a Russo-Chinese alliance—assuming that the Chinese would want it—Russia would be the junior partner, with potentially negative territorial consequences eventually for Russia itself.

Still other Russians cherish dreams of a Slavic Union under the aegis of the Kremlin, involving Ukraine and Belarus and enjoying "a privileged role" in the space of the former Russian empire and of the Soviet Union. They underestimate in that context the contagious appeal of nationalism, especially among the younger Ukrainians and Belarusians who have recently savored their new sovereign status. Notions of a "common economic space" with a dominant Russia cannot hide the fact that its hypothetical economic benefits cannot override the proud feelings of distinctive national identity and political independence. Efforts

FIGURE 4.1 GLOBAL PERFORMANCE RANKINGS AND GLOBAL DEMOGRAPHIC RANKINGS FOR TURKEY AND RUSSIA

Global Performance Rankings for Turkey and Russia

VARIABLE	TURKEY'S RANK	COUNTRY RANKED ABOVE AND BELOW TURKEY	RUSSIA'S RANK	COUNTRY RANKED ABOVE AND BELOW RUSSIA
Political Freedom[1]	Partly Free		Not Free	
Freedom of the Press[2]	101st	Tied with 3 other countries including Albania	174th	173rd Yemen, 175th Congo
International Trade Logistics[3]	39th	38th Slovak Republic, 40th Saudi Arabia	94th	93rd Georgia, 95th Tanzania
Human Development[4]	79th	78th Peru, 80th Ecuador	71st	70th Albania, 72nd Macedonia
Education[5]	109th	108th Saudi Arabia, 110th St. Vincent and the Grenadines	42nd	41st Switzerland, 43rd Bulgaria
Environmental Performance[6]	77th	76th Armenia, 78th Iran	69th	68th Egypt, 70th Argentina
Economic Competitiveness[7]	61st	60th Slovak Republic, 62nd Sri Lanka	63rd	62nd Sri Lanka, 64th Uruguay
Perceived Governmental Corruption[8]	56th	Tied with Malaysia and Namibia	154th	146th Yemen, 164th Democratic Republic of the Congo (9 tied with Russia at 154th)
Entrepreneurship[9]	43rd	42nd South Africa, 44th Mexico	57th	56th Thailand, 58th Tunisia

NOTES

1.Freedom House's *Freedom in the World Report 2010.*

2. Freedom House's *Freedom of the Press Report 2009.*

3. World Bank's *Logistics Performance Index (LPI) 2010.*

4. UNDP's *Human Development Index (HDI) 2009.*

5. UNDP's *Education Index 2009.*

6. *Environmental Performance Index (EPI) 2010.*

7. World Economic Forum's *Global Competitiveness Index (GCI) 2010—2011.*

8. Transparency International's *Corruption Perceptions Index (CPI) 2010.*

9. Acs-Szerb Global Entrepreneurship and Development Index *(GEDI) 2010.*

Global Demographic Rankings for Turkey and Russia[10]

DEMOGRAPHIC CATEGORY	TURKEY'S RANK	NUMBER	RUSSIA'S RANK	NUMBER
Population	17th	77,804,122 million	9th	139,390,205 million
Population Growth Rate	97th	1.272%	222nd	-0.465%
Birth Rate	107th	18.28 births/1,000 population	176th	11.11 births/1,000 population
Death Rate	164th (low)	6.1 deaths/1,000 population	7th (high)	16.04 deaths/1,000 population
Life Expectancy at Birth	126th	72.23 years	161st	66.16 years
Total Fertility Rate	115th	2.18 children born/woman	200th	1.41 children born/woman
HIV/AIDS Adult Prevalence Rate	155th (low)	Less than 0.1%	52nd (high)	1.1%
People Living with AIDS	NA	NA	13th	940,000
Deaths from AIDS	NA	NA	13th	40,000/year

10. CIA World Fact Book 2010 estimates.

to pressure Ukraine or Belarus into a Slavic "union" thus risk entangling Russia in prolonged conflicts with its immediate neighbors.

Finally, Moscow's relationship with the West is still burdened by Russia's ambiguous relationship with its Stalinist past. Unlike Germany, which has repudiated in toto the Nazi chapter of its history, Russia has both officially denounced and yet still respects the individuals most directly responsible for some of history's most bloody crimes. Lenin's embalmed remains continue to be honored in a mausoleum that overlooks the Red Square in Moscow and Stalin's ashes are installed in the nearby Kremlin wall. (Anything similar for Hitler in Berlin would surely discredit Germany's democratic credentials.) An unresolved ambiguity thus persists, reflected in the absence of a clear-cut indictment of Lenin's and Stalin's regimes in officially approved history schoolbooks. Official unwillingness to fully confront head-on the ugly Soviet past, epitomized in Putin's own equivocations on this subject and his nostalgia for Soviet grandeur, has obstructed Russia's progress toward democracy while burdening Russia's relations with its most immediate Western neighbors.

Therefore, a Russia left to its own devices, and not deliberately drawn into a larger democratically transformative framework, could again become a source of tension and occasionally even a security threat to some of its neighbors.* Lacking leadership with the strength and the will to modernize, increasingly aware of its relative social retardation (with only Moscow and St. Petersburg regions matching the West's

---

* In late spring of 2007, Estonia was the object of massive cyberattacks from unknown sources following the dismantling in its capital of a statue honoring the Soviet army. In 2009, Russia held a major military exercise on the western borders, called Zapad ("the West"), simulating a counterattack against a Western invader (otherwise unidentified), which culminated in a simulated nuclear attack on the capital of a Western neighbor (also unidentified). Despite the occasional Russo-Chinese flirtation and economic cooperation, Russia in 2010 conducted major military maneuvers in eastern Siberia, called Vostok ("the East") simulating a major conflict with a likewise unnamed enemy threatening Russia's far-eastern territorial integrity.

standards of living), still uneasy regarding China's growing global power, resentful of America's continuing worldwide preeminence, proud of its vast and resource-rich territory, anxious over the depopulation of its far east and its general demographic crisis, and alert to the growing cultural and religious alienation of its Muslim population, Russia remains unable to define for itself a stable role that strikes a realistic balance between its ambitions and its actual potential.

Thus, in the short run, the currently entrenched Russian power elites—connected with the traditional coercive institutions of the state, nostalgic for the imperial past, and appealing to nationalistic notions deeply entrenched in the public—are an impediment to pro-Western gravitation. In fact, Putin—who could replace Medvedev as President in 2012, or in the least restrict Medvedev's more ambitious democratic desires—has been quite frank that in his view Russia's needed modernization should be a joint Russian-European project, to the exclusion of America and unrelated to democratization. Appealing directly to German business interests (in a personal message alluringly entitled "An Economic Community from Lisbon to Vladivostok," *Süddeutsche Zeitung,* November 25, 2010), Putin made it clear—in contrast to Medvedev's emphasis on democratization—that in his view Europe's, and especially Germany's, involvement in Russia's modernization would be profitable for the Europeans but it would not be premised on Russia's political Westernization.

Given the urgency of Russia's internal problems and depending on what choice Russia makes, the next decade—as already noted—could be decisive for Russia's future and, indirectly, for the prospects of a more vital and larger democratic West. Unfortunately, Putin's vision of that future is a backward-looking combination of assertive nationalism, thinly veiled hostility toward America for its victory in the Cold War, and nostalgia for both modernity and superpower status (financed, he hopes, by Europe). The state he wishes to shape bears a striking resemblance to Italy's experiment with Fascism: a highly authoritarian (but not totalitarian) state involving a symbiotic relationship between its power elite and its business oligarchy, with its ideology based on thinly disguised and bombastic chauvinism.

Coolheaded realism, therefore, dictates caution regarding the declarations of some Russian policy advocates who publicly proclaim a desire for closer ties even with NATO. Private conversations with Moscow's "think tankers" confirm that such advocacy is often guided by the reasonable assumption that any prompt movement in such direction would in fact advance the more familiar Russian objective of rendering NATO largely impotent. A more vulnerable Europe would then be easier to pick apart and its internal diversity exploited to the advantage of Russia's more traditional national interests.

It follows from the foregoing that the argument made by some Europeans (often connected with commercial circles in Germany and Italy) that a prompt enlargement of NATO to include Russia would provide a shortcut to a grand accommodation is misguided. It would most likely produce the reverse. Russia's entry, in its current authoritarian as well as highly corrupted political condition and with its military's obsessively secretive mindset, would simply mean the end of NATO as an integrated alliance of democratic states. Much the same could be said if Russia were to become a part of the EU without first undergoing the required vigorous constitutional adaptation to Europe's democratic standards that Turkey is currently trying to satisfy. Genuinely closer relations are not likely to be achieved by a commercial stampede driven by Western European businessmen (not to mention some former statesmen), anxious to capitalize on Russia's resources while indifferent to the importance of shared values in developing a lasting relationship.

There are, however, also some hopeful signs that the needed and potentially historic geopolitical reorientation regarding Russia's long-term future is incubating among its upper strata. Russia's domestic retardation increasingly validates the anxieties of the Russian Westernizers, located mainly in Moscow's increasingly numerous think tanks and its mass media, that Russia is falling behind. Spreading awareness of that retardation increases Russia's potential susceptibility to a historically visionary but strategically prudent long-term Western outreach.

The unexpected surfacing in late 2009 of Dmitry Medvedev, Putin's handpicked replacement, as the most prominent spokesman for the modernization=democratization school of thought signaled the growing legitimacy of such views in Russia's evolving political spectrum. Views that hitherto were confined to mostly intellectual dissenters thus began to percolate at the highest levels. Even if it eventually turns out that Putin reclaims the presidency, or that Medvedev ceases to press his case in the political arena, the very fact that the President of Russia could declare that in his view Western-type modernization of Russia (which he strongly advocates) inherently requires democratization was a milestone in Russia's political evolution. In October 2010, during his private exchange of views in Moscow with this writer, Medvedev was even more outspoken.

It is now evident that there is in today's Russia a growing constituency of people—admittedly, still mainly in the elites of the key urban centers of Moscow and St. Petersburg—who are attracted to Medvedev's vision of modernization. They include not only the intellectuals, but also the growing thousands of graduates of Western institutions of higher learning, the millions who travel to the West, and the increasing number of entrepreneurs with ties and interests involving the West. Moreover, the Russian mass media, especially TV, both in mass entertainment and in more serious programs, now project the Western life-style as the norm. Last but by no means least, the daily press is generally nonideological, though Russia's wounded imperial hubris more than occasionally slants news reportage about America.

Ultimately, it is up to the Russians to decide whether they wish to take advantage of their territorial and cultural proximity with the West, and their oft-noted social affinity for America, to link deliberately their efforts at social modernization with genuine Western-type political democratization. Russia's intellectual elite increasingly recognizes the interdependence of these two processes; its business elite has belatedly

On September 10, 2009, the official web portal of the President of Russia released for public consumption Medvedev's statement entitled "Go Russia!" It contained such a remarkably scathing indictment of Russia's shortcomings and such a bold call for reforms that some excerpts from it deserve citation:

> Our current economy still reflects the major flaw of the Soviet system: it largely ignores individual needs. . . . Centuries of corruption have debilitated Russia from time immemorial. Until today this corrosion has been due to the excessive government presence in many significant aspects of economic and other social activities. . . . The impressive legacy of the two greatest modernizations in our country's history—that of Peter the Great (imperial) and the Soviet one—unleashed ruin, humiliation and resulted in the deaths of millions of our countrymen. . . . Only our own experience of democratic endeavor will give us the right to say: we are free, we are responsible, we are successful. Democracy needs to be protected. The fundamental rights and freedoms of our citizens must be as well. They need to be protected primarily from the sort of corruption that breeds tyranny, lack of freedom, and injustice. . . . Nostalgia should not guide our foreign policy and our strategic long-term goal is Russia's modernization. [One can only wonder whom Medvedev had in mind when making his pointed reference to "nostalgia" in foreign policy.]

become more aware of it after the financial crisis of 2007, while its power elite is increasingly worried that Russia's development lags dramatically behind that of the emerging global colossus to its east. The gradually spreading Russian consensus regarding the cumulatively negative implications of the foregoing thus justifies cautious optimism concerning the longer-term prospects of a more stable and increasingly binding East-West relationship even in the face of Russia's still-unsettled internal political power dynamics.

Accordingly, if it can be said that Europe is still unfinished business without a deeper and more extensive relationship with Russia, it can also be said that Russia will lack a secure geopolitical future as well as a self-satisfying modern and democratic identity without a closer connection with the West in general and with Europe specifically. Without a confidence-building and increasingly transformative accommodation with the West, Russia is likely to remain too weak internally and too conflicted in its external ambitions to become a truly successful democratic state. The September 2009 statement by Medvedev thus was not only a timely and stark warning to his countrymen; it was also a definition of the only real option open to Russia: "Our current domestic, financial, and technological capabilities are not sufficient for a qualitative improvement in the quality of life. We need money and technology from Europe, America, and Asia. In turn, these countries need the opportunities that Russia offers. We are very interested in the rapprochement and interpenetration of our culture and economies."

A partnership both stimulated and facilitated by Russia's political modernization offers the best hope for genuine collaboration. That is more likely to happen if the West also sustains its transatlantic unity and on that basis pursues a long-term policy characterized by strategic clarity and historic outreach to Russia. Strategic clarity means nothing less than a realistic assessment as to what kind of Russia would enhance—and not divide—the West. Historic outreach means that the process of the West and of Russia growing together has to be pursued both patiently and persistently if it is to become truly enduring. The cardinal principle of a strategically minded and historically prudent policy has to be that only a Europe linked to America can confidently reach eastward to embrace Russia in a historically binding relationship.

A congruence of external interests and a commitment to shared values within the framework of a constitutional democracy between the West and Russia are both required. A progressive adoption by Russia of universal democratic standards (pursued through the "interpenetration"—to use Medvedev's word—of a common culture) would entail a gradually deepening transformation of Russia's internal political arrangements over time. And externally, it would facilitate a steady expansion of social, economic, and eventually political ties with the West. A free trade zone, freedom of travel throughout Europe, and, eventually, open opportunities for personal resettlement whenever a legitimate economic interest beckons, could catalyze changes within Russia compatible with deeper political and security links to the West.

In order to speculate how long it would take Russia to evolve into a seamless part of the West, it is useful to bear in mind the dramatic transformation of global geopolitical realities that has occurred in just the last forty years and the fact that we live in a time characterized by the dramatic acceleration of history. (Figure 4.2 provides a highly capsulated summary of the sweeping geopolitical changes that have occurred in the course of only forty years, between 1970 and 2010.)

A systematically nurtured closer relationship between Russia and the Atlantic West (economically with the EU, and in security matters with NATO and with the United States more generally) could be hastened by gradual Russian acceptance of a truly independent Ukraine, which desires more urgently than Russia to be close to Europe and eventually to be a member of the European Union. Hence the EU was wise in November 2010 to grant Ukraine access to its programs, pointing toward a formal association agreement in 2011. A Ukraine not hostile to Russia but somewhat ahead of it in its access to the West actually helps to encourage Russia's movement Westward toward a potentially rewarding European future. On the other hand, a Ukraine isolated from the West and increasingly politically subordinated to Russia would encourage Russia's unwise choice in favor of its imperial past.

The precise nature of the more formal and binding institutional ties between the West and Russia that could evolve over the next several decades is, unavoidably at this stage, a matter largely of speculation. To the extent possible such a process should move forward in a balanced fashion simultaneously on social and economic as well as political and security levels. One can envisage expanding arrangements for social interactions, increasingly similar legal and constitutional arrangements, joint security exercises between NATO and the Russian military, as well as the development of new coordinating policy institutions within

FIGURE 4.2 THE UNPREDICTABILITY OF HISTORICAL DISCONTINUITY FROM 1970 TO 2010

	ATLANTIC ALLIANCE	SOVIET UNION (RUSSIA)	CHINA
Circa Decade 1970–1980	Alliance covers only half of Europe Europe is concerned about growing Soviet military buildup US bogged down in Vietnam, which it later abandons	Recently occupied Czechoslovakia (1968) Large-scale strategic buildup threatens to surpass US's Proclaimed its expectation to surpass US in economic might by 1980	Domestic turmoil because of widespread political violence produced by the Cultural Revolution Massive purges of political elite Manufacturing roughly 9% of the US
Circa Decade 1980–1990	Pro-US Shah overthrown in Iran US normalizes relations with China and they form a tacit anti-Soviet alliance	Soviet Union invades Afghanistan Poised to invade Poland and crush Solidarity Experiments with "perestroika" in face of economic slowdown	Adopts liberalizing economic reforms under Deng Xiaoping Normalizes relations with the US and collaborates with the US against the USSR in Afghanistan Quells democratic protests in Tiananmen Square
Circa Decade 1990–2000	US emerges from the Cold War as sole super power Reunification of Germany European community becomes European Union NATO expands to Central Europe	Solidarity in Poland takes power and the Soviet Bloc collapses Soviet Union disintegrates and former Soviet Republics gain independence Russia experiments with democracy amid social crisis	Expands economic reform from rural areas to urban centers Achieves close to 10% annual economic growth Launches urban infrastructural renovation
Circa Decade 2000–2010	US undertakes "war on terror" after 9/11 US overthrows Taliban in Afghanistan US invades Iraq in 2003 EU expands to Central Europe The West experiences a large-scale financial meltdown US enters systematic crisis because of debt and domestic economic slowdown	Russia engages in war in Chechnya Pursues an authoritarian restoration of state power under Putin Seeks to become an energy superpower Russian economy shows itself to be vulnerable to global trends and social stagnation persists	Enters the World Trade Organization Emerges as the industrial factory of the world surpassing the US in manufacturing, and as the world's second-largest economy 250 million strong middle class emerges as a consequence of 30 years of economic growth

such an evolving larger West, all resulting in Russia's increasing readiness for eventual membership in the EU.

But even short of Russia's actual membership in the EU, the emerging geopolitical community of interest between the United States, Europe, and Russia (from Vancouver eastward to Vladivostok) could in the meantime lead to a formal framework for ongoing consultations regarding common policies. Since any Westward gravitation by Russia would likely be accompanied (or even preceded) by a similar accommodation with Ukraine, the institutional seat of such a collective consultative organ (or perhaps in the meantime the Council of Europe) could be located in Kyiv (the ancient capital of the Kyivan Rus', which a thousand years ago had regal ties with the West). Its location in Europe's current east, and just north of Turkey, would symbolize the West's renewed vitality and enlarging territorial scope.

Looking beyond 2025, it is therefore not unrealistic to conceive of a larger configuration of the West. Turkey could by then already be a full member of the EU, perhaps having moved to that stage by some intermediary arrangements regarding the more difficult requirements of EU membership. But with Europe and America guided by an intelligent and strategically deliberate vision of a larger West, the process of Turkey's inclusion in Europe should be sustainable even if not rapidly consummated in the short term. It is also reasonable to assume that in the course of the next two or more decades a genuinely cooperative and binding arrangement between the West and Russia could be attained—under optimal circumstances resulting eventually even in Russia's membership in both the EU and NATO—if in the meantime Russia does embark on a truly comprehensive law-based democratic transformation compatible with EU as well as NATO standards.

For all concerned, that would be a win-win outcome. It would be in keeping with the underlying pressures of history, social change, and modernization. For Turkey, and for Russia more specifically, it would firmly cement their places in the modern democratic world, while Ukraine's inclusion would ensure its national independence. For today's

Europe, it would offer tempting new vistas of opportunity and adventure. Attracted by open spaces and new entrepreneurial opportunities, Europe's young would be challenged "to go east," be it to northeast Siberia or to eastern Anatolia. The uninhibited movement of people and the availability of new challenges could give a lift to Europe's current vision, which is presently so focused inward on matters pertaining to social security. Modern highways and high-speed rail crisscrossing trans-Eurasia would encourage population shifts, with the declining Russian presence in the Far East reinvigorated by an economically and demographically dynamic inflow from the West. Within a few years, an increasingly cosmopolitan Vladivostok could become a European city without ceasing to be part of Russia.

A larger European framework that involves in varying ways Turkey and Russia would mean that Europe, still allied with America, could become in effect a globally critical player. The resulting bigger West—sharing a common space and common principles—would be better positioned to offset the tendencies in some parts of Eurasia toward religious intolerance, political fanaticism, or rising nationalistic hostility by offering a more attractive economic and political alternative.

However, a larger and more vital West needs to be more than a renewal of historical confidence in the universal relevance of Western democratic values. It must be the result of a deliberate effort by both America and Europe to embrace more formally Turkey as well as Russia in a larger framework of cooperation based on such shared values and on their genuine democratic commitment. Getting there will take time, perseverance, and—in the more complicated and thus more difficult case of Russia—coolheaded realism. It would represent in any case a giant step forward in the historical progression of a continent that in the last century has been the locale for history's greatest mass slaughters, for debilitating and destructive wars, and for the most organized expressions of mankind's capacity for cruelty to itself. Considering how dramatically global politics have changed in the course of the last forty years (see Figure 4.2), in the age of historical acceleration such a vision

MAP 4.1 BEYOND 2025: A LARGER WEST— THE CORE OF GLOBAL STABILITY

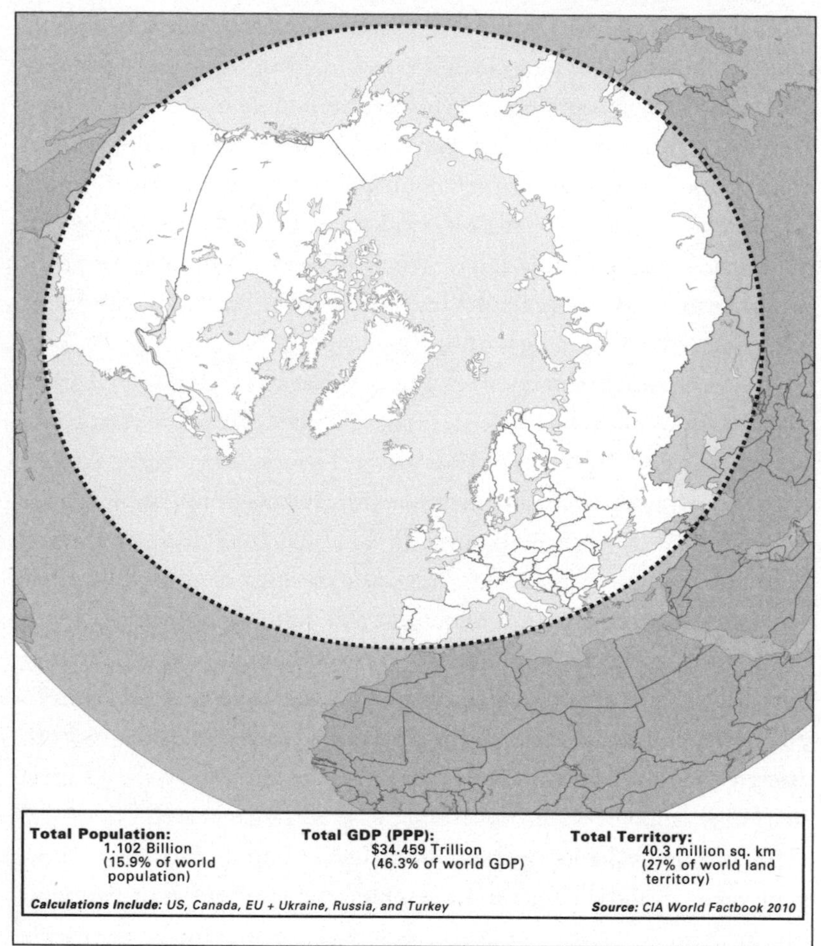

of a geopolitically larger and a more vital West becoming a reality during the second quarter of the twenty-first century could actually turn out to be an overly cautious glimpse into the future.

3: A Stable and Cooperative New East

Given the ongoing shift of global power from the West to the East, will the new Asia of the twenty-first century become like the old Europe of the twentieth, obsessed with interstate rivalry and eventually the victim of self-destruction? If so, the consequences for global peace would be catastrophic. Hence this question has to be asked at the outset, especially since at first glance the similarities between the Asia of today and the Europe of yesterday seem striking.

In the early twentieth century, Europe stood at the apex of its global influence, but within a mere thirty years it self-destructed. The precipitating cause was the difficulty of accommodating the rise of an assertive and increasingly powerful imperial Germany within the existing European system. Thence some similarity to the challenges posed by the rise of contemporary China in today's new Asia. France, resentful of its defeat by Prussia in 1870, opposed Germany's rise and was alarmed by it. Some contemporary parallels with India thus come to mind. Offshore, but very influential in Europe, was Great Britain, not directly involved in European affairs but certainly concerned by them. In that regard, some analogy with contemporary Japan also suggests itself. Last but not least, Russia was also involved. Its opposition to Germany's support of Austria-Hungary against Serbia ignited the First World War in 1914, and its collaboration with Germany in 1939 produced the second and final round in Europe's self-destruction. Today's Russia, worried by China, is sympathetic to India as a counterweight to China.

The major impulse for the European catastrophe was the inability of the European interstate system (shaped largely a century earlier by the grand imperial bargain contrived in the Congress of Vienna in

1815) to handle the simultaneous rise of a new imperial power and to satisfy the effervescent aspirations of populist nationalisms throughout Central Europe, which became more intense over the course of the subsequent decades. In today's world, in which Europe is no longer the center, the issue of Asia's regional stability is obviously of crucial relevance to global well-being. That is so not only because of China's climb to international preeminence, but also because of the self-evident importance of Japan, India, Indonesia, and South Korea in the global economic hierarchy, not to mention the cumulative economic weight of the several medium-sized Southeast Asian states. Measured together—even if they do not all act in concert—the Asian states account for 24.7% of global GNP and 54% of global population.

Moreover, as noted in Part 1, the huge Asian portion of the world's population is now largely politically awakened. Its political awareness is defined and energized by nationalism and/or religion, each infused with varying degrees (depending on specific historical experiences of the individual countries) of lingering anti-Western resentments. The common thread in their respective—if varying—historical narratives is the theme of anti-imperialism, with specific segments of the West held accountable for past real or imagined abuses. In brief, the East is not one—and politically, religiously, culturally, and ethnically it is more diverse than the hesitantly unifying West. The East's political awakening is more recent and its bitter memories fresher. The East is collectively proud and increasingly rich as well as powerful, but its huge populations are still mostly poor, crowded, and deprived. And many of the countries in the East are hostile toward one another. Their populist energies are volatile while the intensity of their nationalisms is reminiscent of Europe's during the previous century and a half.

Asian nationalisms, especially if reinforced in some cases by religious fervor, are thus a major threat to the political stability of the region. They could also become a major impediment to the emergence and/or consolidation of genuinely stable democracies, especially if their potentially explosive appeal is triggered by some emotive incidents in interstate relations over a variety of conflicting issues. Unleashed passions, politically ignited by nationalistic slogans, could generate pressures that even the region's authoritarian regimes could not resist. Still worse, its few existing relatively democratic systems might have no choice but to embrace aroused nationalistic expectations as evidence of their own populist solidarity.

In that potentially menacing context, the possibilities of conflict are many. Some could arise out of intensifying regional power rivalries, with that of China and India being the obvious example. Disputes over water rights or borders could provide both the pretext and the spark. Some—as in the case of Pakistan and India—could be triggered by unresolved and potentially explosive territorial conflicts that could then unleash violent nationalistic and religious hatreds to the point of threatening respective national survival. Some could be the unintended products of lingering historical enmity, as in the case of Japan and China. Some could simply be the by-products of internal instabilities and of human miscalculation at the highest level; clearly the attitude of North Korea toward South Korea comes to mind. Some could also be triggered by overlapping maritime claims, as between China and Japan, as well as between China and its Southeast Asian neighbors next to the South China Sea. In addition, a declining Russia that fails to Westernize and thus to modernize, could also be resentful of the increasingly effective Chinese efforts to expand its access to the natural resources of Mongolia and of the new Central Asian states.

Very serious international tensions could also result from a reciprocal failure by America and China to adjust cooperatively to the changing distribution of political and economic power in their bilateral relationship. Specific precipitating issues—in addition to the obvious economic rivalry and persistent financial disputes—might involve the status of Taiwan, or the extent of the American naval presence in the proximity of Chinese territorial waters, or conflicting interests in a Korean conflict.

Finally, one has to consider the potential impact of nuclear weapons on these regional contests. The new East already includes three overt nuclear powers (China, India, and Pakistan), as well as a less transparent

MAP 4.2 POTENTIAL ASIAN CONFLICTS

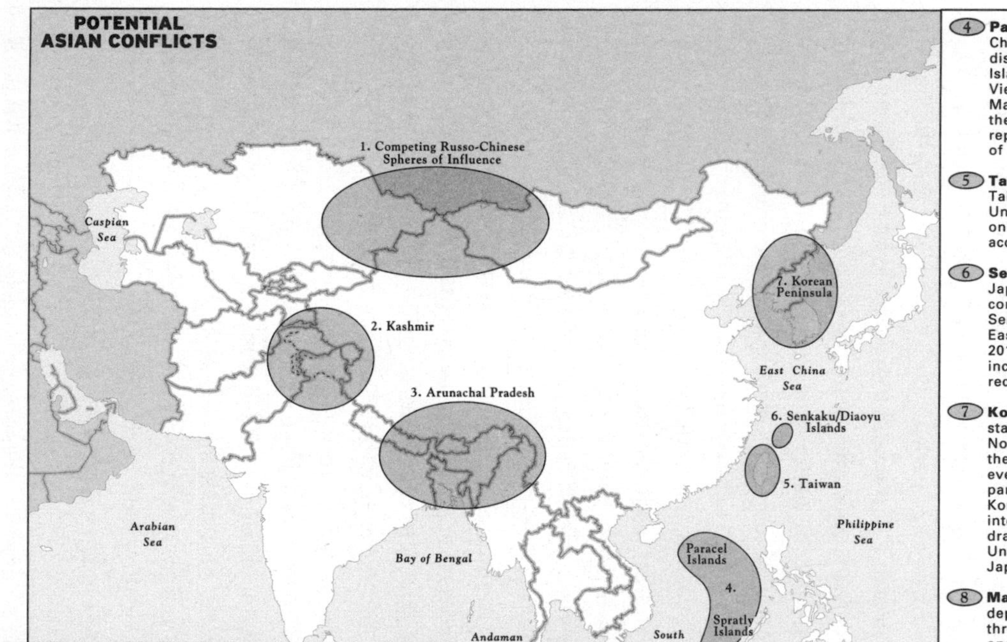

fourth, North Korea, which periodically both postures and threatens as a self-proclaimed nuclear power. If uncertain of American security commitments, Japan could very quickly become a significant nuclear power as well, while on the southwestern fringes of the new Asia, Iran may already be in the process of acquiring nuclear weapons. The absence of any larger framework of collective security in Asia (of the kind that exists in today's Europe) and the potential of so many possible conflicts erupting in a setting of such volatile nationalistic aspirations justifies concerns that, at some point, an international incident could spark a larger regional outbreak on a scale that—especially if nuclear weapons were employed—could match or even overshadow the horrors that Europe experienced in the previous century.

But, in spite of the multitude of uncertainties and asymmetries in Asia, the arguments in support of the proposition that the new East is doomed to destructive international warfare fall short of being conclusive. Though the similarities with twentieth-century Europe may seem compelling, the differences—derived from the novelty of twenty-first-century global realities and from the unique history of the Asian interstate system—are equally meaningful.

First is the geopolitical fact that—unlike the Europe of the early twentieth century, which was still then the center of world power—Asia currently is not or at least is not yet the center of world military power. That means that any Asian leader, in considering major warfare, has to take into account the possibility of intervention by indirectly affected outside powers. For example, in the case of a truly significant war (and not merely a border skirmish) between India and China, Russia would almost certainly decide to help India in some fashion simply because that would weaken China. America's reactions would probably be calibrated by concerns that no one power should emerge as the decisive Asian potentate. Hence America, in order to avoid a one-sided outcome, would be likely to strive to reduce the scale of respective war aims as well as the scope and intensity of violence between the protagonists.

Awareness among the ruling Asian elites of the reality of more powerful potential external protagonists may in part be the reason why the military budgets of the Asian countries are relatively low in relationship to their respective GDPs. (According to the Word Bank, China spends 2%, India 3%, and Japan 1% of their GDPs on the military. The United States spends 4.6%.) Even in the cases of China and India, their military spending and their relatively modest nuclear arsenals suggest that neither side is seriously contemplating the possibility of a decisive resolution by the use of force to their existing or potential differences—continuing national suspicions of each other notwithstanding.

Second, contemporary Asia thrives now in a setting of worldwide commercial interdependence, which not only inhibits reliance on unilateral military action but also creates opportunities for alternative sources of self-gratification and of the fulfillment of national aspirations, such as through economic growth spurred by foreign trade, thereby dampening nationalistic extremism. China certainly is aware of the fact that the remarkable thirty-year-long transformation of its domestic socioeconomic conditions has gained it international preeminence as well as remarkable economic-financial standing. And China's experience is not unique. Other increasingly successful Asian states (notably South Korea and the ASEAN bloc) benefit from a web of connections and relationships that induce some degree of restraint over nationalistic irrationality. Their twenty-first-century middle classes tend to be interconnected with the world, to a degree that their twentieth-century European predecessors never were. Study abroad, frequent travel, business interconnections, shared professional aspirations, and the intimacy of transnational contact through the Internet all contribute to an outlook not immune, to be sure, to nationalistic appeals but nonetheless more conscious of their interdependent self-interest.

Third, the historical contrast between Europe and Asia also deserves recognition. As noted in a remarkable study of China's emergence, already some centuries ago "the most important states of East Asia—from Japan, Korea, and China to Vietnam, Laos, Thailand, and Kampuchea . . . had all been linked to one another, directly or through the Chinese center, by trade and diplomatic relations and held together by a shared understanding of the principles, norms, and rules that regulated their mutual interactions. . . . Long periods of peace among the European powers were the exception rather than the rule. . . . In sharp contrast . . . the national states of the East Asian system were almost uninterruptedly at peace, not for 100 but 300 years."[3]

Finally, the motivating impulse of the threats to peace in the Asia of the twenty-first century likewise tends to be different from Europe's of the twentieth century. In the latter case, much of the impetus for interstate warfare was the product of nationalistically aroused territorial ambitions of nation-states motivated by notions that more territory equals more power equals greater status. In its most extreme rendition, such aspirations were justified by spurious concepts of living space ("lebensraum") allegedly needed for national survival. In contemporary Asia, internal conflicts derived from ethnic diversity and pre-nation-state tribal loyalties rather than external territorial ambitions are more likely to be the main cause of regional instability. Indeed, with the exception of Pakistan's fears of India, the preservation of the stability of the existing states rather than concerns over territorial designs from their neighbors may currently be the more serious preoccupation of most of the military commands in the southeast and southwest Asian states.

In the most important case of the very populous India, regional turmoil could ensue from that country's two potentially disruptive internal contradictions: between the very rich and the extremely poor, with the poverty in India more acute than in China, and from the ethnic-linguistic-religious diversity of Indian society. Unlike China, in which the Han Chinese account for 91.5% of the population, the largest ethnic group in India accounts for about 70%, which means that as many as 300 million people are in effect ethnic minorities. In terms of religion, the Hindus account for around 950 million Indians, with the Muslims numbering approximately 160 million, the Sikhs about 22 million, and others in a larger variety. Less than one-half of the population shares a common language, Hindi. Moreover, literacy levels in India are appallingly low, with the majority of women actually illiterate. Rural unrest is rising and has not been contained in spite of percolating violence for more than a decade.

Moreover, the Indian political system has yet to prove that it can function as "the world's largest democracy." That test will take place when its population becomes truly politically awakened and engaged. Given the country's very high levels of public illiteracy as well as the connection between privilege and wealth at the top of the political establishment, India's current "democratic" process is rather reminiscent of the British aristocratic "democracy," prior to the appearance of trade unions, in the second half of the nineteenth century. The operational viability of the existing system will be truly tested when the heterogeneous public at large becomes both politically conscious and assertive. Ethnic, religious, and linguistic differences could then threaten India's internal cohesion. Should they escalate out of control, the neighboring Pakistan, already challenged by tribal unrest, could also become the geopolitical focus of a broader regional violence.

In that potentially conflicted setting, the stability of Asia will depend in part on how America responds to two overlapping regional triangles centered around China. The first pertains to China, India, and Pakistan. The second pertains to China, Japan, and Korea, with the Southeast Asian states playing a supporting role. In the case of the former, Pakistan could be the major point of contention and the precipitating source of instability. In the case of the latter, Korea (both South and North) and/or possibly also Taiwan could become the foci of insecurity.

In both cases, the United States is still the key player, with the capacity to alter balances and affect outcomes. It therefore needs to be stated at the outset that the United States should be guided by the general principle that any direct US military involvement in conflicts between rival Asian powers should be avoided. No outcome of either a Pakistani-Indian war, or of one also involving China, or even of a strictly Chinese-Indian war is likely to produce consequences more damaging to US interests than a renewed and possibly expanded American military engagement on the Asian mainland. And the latter could even precipitate a wider chain reaction of ethnic and religious instability in Asia.

The above obviously does not apply to existing US treaty obligations to Japan and South Korea, where US forces are actually deployed. Moreover, US noninvolvement in possible conflicts among Asian states themselves should not imply indifference to their potential outcomes. The United States should certainly use its international influence to discourage the outbreak of warfare, to help contain it if it does occur, and to avoid a one-sided outcome as its conclusion. But such efforts should entail the participation of other powers potentially also affected by any major regional instability in Asia. Some of them may even prefer America to become involved while they benefit from remaining on the sidelines. Hence the needed attempts to prevent or to contain the crisis and to impose, if necessary, some costs on the more aggressive party should not be America's responsibility alone.

The first triangle involves competition for Asian primacy. China and India are already major players on the international scene. India is the world's most populous country; its economy is on a takeoff; its formal democratic structure and its future viability as a possible alternative to China's authoritarian model is of special interest to democratic America. China is already the world's number two economic power, before too long that is likely to be the case (and in some respects it already may be so) with regard to its military capacity, and it is rapidly emerging as an ascending global power. Thus, the Chinese-Indian relationship is inherently competitive and antagonistic, with Pakistan being the regional point of contention.

On India's side, the existing tensions and reciprocal national animosities are fueled by the relatively uninhibited hostility toward China expressed in India's uncensored media and in India's strategic discussions. Invariably, China is presented in them as a threat, most often territorial in nature, and India's publications frequently make reference to China's 1962 occupation by force of disputed borderline territories. China's efforts to establish an economic and political presence in

Myanmar's and in Pakistan's Indian Ocean ports are presented to the public as a strategic design to encircle India. The Chinese mass media, under official control, are more restrained in their pronouncements but purposefully patronize India as a not-so-serious rival, further inflaming negative Indian sentiments.

To a considerable extent, such Chinese feelings of aloofness toward India are derived from China's superior societal performance. Its GNP is considerably larger than India's, its urban modernization and infrastructural innovation are far more advanced, and its population is considerably more literate as well as ethnically and linguistically more homogenous (see Figure 4.3 on pp. 166–167).

In any case, both sides are the strategic captives of their subjective feelings and of their geopolitical contexts. The Indians envy the Chinese economic and infrastructural transformation. The Chinese are contemptuous of India's relative backwardness (on the social level most dramatically illustrated by asymmetrical levels of literacy of their respective populations) and of its lack of discipline. The Indians fear Chinese-Pakistani collusion; the Chinese feel vulnerable to India's potential capacity to interfere with Chinese access through the Indian Ocean to the Middle East and Africa. Apart from ritualistic reiteration in diplomatic communiqués of a shared commitment to peace, influential private voices are rarely heard advocating a comprehensive mutual accommodation, and so reciprocal disdain lingers and grows.

America's role in this rivalry should be cautious and detached. A prudent US policy, especially in regard to an alliance with India, should not however be interpreted as indifference to India's potential role as an alternative to China's authoritarian political model. India offers such promise for the future, especially if it succeeds in combining sustained development with more pervasive democracy. Hence cordiality in relations with India is justified, though it should not imply support on such contentious issues as Kashmir, given that India's record in that instance is open to criticism, nor imply that a cooperative relationship with India is aimed at China.

Given that some policy circles in the United States have started to advocate a formal US-India alliance, presumably against China and in effect also against Pakistan, it also needs to be stated explicitly that any such undertaking would be contrary to US national security interests. It would increase the likelihood of US involvement in potentially prolonged and bitter Asian conflicts. The unwise US decision of 2011 to sell advanced weaponry to India, in contrast to the ongoing embargo on arms sales to China, while also enhancing India's nuclear programs is already earning the United States the hostility of the Chinese by conveying the impression that America sees China as its enemy even before China itself had decided to be America's enemy.

Moreover, a US-India alliance would be a gratis favor to Russia without any Russian favor in return. In fact, such an alliance would be inimical in two significant ways to long-term American interests in Eurasia: it would reduce Russian fears of China and thus diminish Russian self-interest in becoming more closely tied to the West, and it would increase Moscow's temptations to take advantage of a distracted America drawn into wider Asian conflicts to assert Russian imperial interests more firmly in Central Asia and in Central Europe. Prospects for a more vital and larger West would thereby become more remote.

Finally, an America-India alliance would also be likely to intensify the appeal of anti-American terrorism among Muslims, who would infer that this partnership was implicitly directed against Pakistan. That would be even more likely if in the meantime religious violence between Hindus and Muslims erupted in parts of India. Much of the rest of the Islamic world, be it in nearby southwest Asia or in Central Asia or in the Middle East, would be roused into mounting sympathy and then support for terrorist acts directed at America. In brief, insofar as the first Asian triangle is concerned, the better part of wisdom is abstention from any alliance that could obligate the United States to military involvement in that part of Asia.

The issue is not so clear-cut with regard to the second regional triangle involving China, Japan, South Korea, and to a lesser degree

FIGURE 4.3 GLOBAL SYSTEMIC PERFORMANCE RANKINGS FOR CHINA AND INDIA, AND INDICATORS OF DEVELOPMENT FOR CHINA AND INDIA

Global Systemic Performance Rankings for China and India

VARIABLE	CHINA'S RANK	COUNTRY RANKED ABOVE AND BELOW CHINA	INDIA'S RANK	COUNTRY RANKED ABOVE AND BELOW INDIA
International Trade Logistics[1]	27th	26th Czech Republic, 28th South Africa	47th	46th Cyprus, 48th Argentina
Human Development[2]	89th	88th Dominican Republic, 90th El Salvador	119th	118th Cape Verde, 120th Timor-Leste
Education[3]	97th	96th Malaysia, 98th Suriname	145th	144th Comoros, 146th Cameroon
Environmental Performance[4]	121st	120th Madagascar, 122nd Qatar	123rd	122nd Qatar, 124th Yemen
Economic Competitiveness[5]	27th	26th Malaysia, 28th Brunei	51st	50th Malta, 52nd Hungary
Perceived Governmental Corruption[6]	78th	73rd Bulgaria, 85th Morocco (5 tied with China at 78th, including Greece)	87th	85th Morocco, 91st Bosnia and Herzegovinia (Albania, Jamaica and Liberia tied with India at 87th)
Entrepreneurship[7]	40th	39th Peru, 41st Colombia	53rd	52nd Panama, 54th Brazil

NOTES

1. World Bank's *Logistics Performance Index (LPI) 2010.*
2. UNDP's *Human Development Index (HDI) 2009.*
3. UNDP's *Education Index 2009.*
4. *Environmental Performance Index (EPI) 2010.*
5. World Economic Forum's *Global Competitiveness Index (GCI) 2010–2011.*
6. Transparency International's *Corruption Perceptions Index (CPI) 2010.*
7. *Acs-Szerb Global Entrepreneurship and Development Index (GEDI) 2010.*

Indicators of Development for China and India[8]

INDICATOR	CHINA'S RANK	NUMBER	INDIA'S RANK	NUMBER
Life Expectancy at Birth	94th	74.51 years	160th	66.46 years
Male Literacy Rate	-	95.7%	-	73.4%
Female Literacy Rate	-	87.6% (2007)	-	47.8% (2001)
Population Living Below PPP $1.25 a day[9]	-	15.9% (2008)	-	41.6% (2008)
Industrial Production Growth Rate	4th	9.9%	8th	9.3%
Investment (Gross Fixed)	1st	46.3% of GDP	13th	32.4% of GDP
Investment in Research and Development (2010)[10]	-	1.4% of GDP (Gross expenditure was $141.4 billion)	-	0.9% of GDP (Gross expenditure was $33.3 billion)
KM of Expressway	-	65,000 km of expressway	-	200 km of expressway

8. CIA World Factbook 2009 and 2010 estimates.

9. UNDP *Human Development Report 2010.* Table 5. Multi-Dimensional Poverty Index.

10. *2011 Global R&D Funding Forecast.* Battelle and R&D Magazine. December 2010.

Southeast Asia. More generally, this issue pertains to China's role as the dominant power on the Asian mainland and to the nature of America's position in the Pacific. Japan is America's key political-military ally in the Far East even though its military capabilities are currently self-restrained, a condition that may be fading because of growing concerns over China's rising power. It is also the world's number three economic power, having only recently been surpassed by China. South Korea is a burgeoning economic power and longtime American ally that relies on the United States to deter any possible conflict with its estranged northern relative. Southeast Asia has less formal ties to the United States and has a strong regional partnership (ASEAN), but it fears the growth of Chinese power. Most importantly, America and China already have an economic relationship that makes both vulnerable to any reciprocal hostility, while the growth of China's economic and political power poses a potential future challenge to America's current global preeminence.

Given China's recent performance, as well as its historical accomplishments, it would be rash to assume that the Chinese economy might suddenly grind to a halt. Back in 1995 (in effect, then at the midpoint of China's now thirty-year-long economic takeoff), some prominent American economists even suggested that by 2010 China might find itself in the same dire straits as the Soviet Union did some thirty years ago after the phantasmagoric official Soviet claims of the 1960s that by 1980 the Soviet Union would surpass America in economic power. By now, it is evident even to the most skeptical that China's economic ascent has been real and that it has a good chance of continuing for a while, though probably at declining annual rates.

That is not to deny that China could be adversely affected by an international decline in demand for Chinese manufactured goods or by a worldwide financial crisis. Also, social tensions in China could rise because of widening social disparities. They could generate political restlessness, of which the historic Tiananmen Square events of 1989 could in some respects be a preview. The new Chinese middle class, now amounting by some counts to about 300 million people, may demand more political rights. But none of that would be reminiscent of the Soviet Union's systemic disaster. China's influential and rising role in world affairs is a reality to which Americans will have to adjust—instead of either demonizing it or engaging in thinly concealed wishful thinking about its failure.

The more serious danger could come from an altogether different source, less economic and more social-political in character. It could surface as the result of a gradual and initially imperceptible decline in the quality of Chinese leadership or of a more perceptible rise in the intensity of Chinese nationalism. Either of the two, or both combined, could produce policies harmful to China's international aspirations and/or could prove disruptive to China's tranquil domestic transformation.

Till now, the performance of the Chinese leadership since the Cultural Revolution has generally been prudent. Deng Xiaoping had vision and determination guided by pragmatic realism. Since Deng, China has gone through three stable leadership renewals thanks, in part, to standardized procedures for firmly scheduled leadership succession. His successors have occasionally differed among themselves (for example, Hu Yaobang, briefly Deng's heir apparent, advocated more political pluralism than was digestible by his comrades). The Chinese leaders have made efforts to anticipate problems, and even to study jointly pertinent foreign experience in tackling the unavoidable complications of domestic policy successes. (In quite a remarkable exercise, the Chinese politburo periodically convenes to study for a whole day some major external or internal issue in order to draw relevant foreign and historical parallels. The very first session dealt, rather revealingly, with the lessons to be learned from the rise and fall of foreign empires, with the most recent identified as being the American.)

The current generation of leaders, no longer revolutionaries or innovators themselves, have thus matured in an established political setting in which the major issues of national policy have been set on a long-term course. Bureaucratic stability—indeed, centralized control—must seem to them to be the only solid foundation for effective government.

But in a highly bureaucratized political setting, conformity, caution, and currying favor with superiors often count for more in advancing a political career than personal courage and individual initiative. Over the longer run, it is questionable whether any political leadership can long remain vital if it is so structured in its personnel policy that it becomes, almost unknowingly, inimical to talent and hostile to innovation. Decay can set in, while the stability of the political system can be endangered if a gap develops between its officially proclaimed orthodoxies and the disparate aspirations of an increasingly politically awakened population.

In the case of China, however, public disaffection is not likely to express itself through a massive quest for democracy but more likely either through social grievances or nationalistic passions. The government is more aware of the former and has been preparing for it. Official planners have even identified publicly and quite frankly the five major threats that in their view could produce mass incidents threatening social stability: (1) disparity between rich and poor, (2) urban unrest and discontent, (3) a culture of corruption, (4) unemployment, and (5) loss of social trust.[4]

The rise of nationalistic passions could prove more difficult to handle. It is already evident, even from officially controlled publications, that intense Chinese nationalism is on the rise. Though the regime in power still advocates caution in the definition of China's standing and historical goals, by 2009 the more serious Chinese media became permeated by triumphalist assertions of China's growing eminence, economic might, and its continued ascent to global preeminence. The potential for a sudden rise in populist passions also became evident in outbursts of demonstrative public anger over some relatively minor naval incidents with Japan near disputed islands. The issue of Taiwan could likewise at some point ignite belligerent public passions against America.

Indeed, the paradox of China's future is that an eventual evolution toward some aspects of democracy may be more feasible under an intelligent but assertive leadership that cautiously channels social pressures for more participation than under an enfeebled leadership that overindulges them. A weakened and gradually more mediocre regime could become tempted by the notion that political unity, as well as its own power, can best be preserved by a policy that embraces the more impatient and more extreme nationalistic definition of China's future. If a leadership fearful of losing its grip on power and declining in vision were to support the nationalist surge, the result could be a disruption of the so far carefully calculated balance between the promotion of China's domestic aspirations and prudent pursuit of China's foreign policy interests.

The foregoing could also precipitate a fundamental change in China's structure of political power. The Chinese army (the People's Liberation Army) is the only nationwide organization capable of asserting national control. It is also heavily involved in the direct management of major economic assets. In the event of a serious decline in the vitality of the existing political leadership and of a rise in populist emotions, the military would most likely assume effective control. Paradoxically, the likelihood of such an eventuality is enhanced by the deliberate politicization of the Chinese officer corps. In the top ranks party membership is 100%. And like the CCP itself, party members in the PLA see themselves as being above the state. In the event of a systemic crisis, for the Communist Party members in uniform the assumption of power would thus be the normal thing to do. And political leadership would thus pass into the hands of a highly motivated, very nationalistic, well-organized, but internationally inexperienced leadership.

An intensely nationalist and militaristic China would generate its own self-isolation. It would dissipate the global admiration for China's modernization and could stimulate residual anti-Chinese public sentiments within the United States, perhaps even with some latent racist overtones. It would be likely to give rise to political pressures for an overly anti-China coalition with whatever Asian nations had become increasingly fearful of Beijing's ambitions. It could transform China's immediate geopolitical neighborhood, currently inclined toward a partnership with the economically successful giant next door, into eager supplicants for external reassurance (preferably from America) against what they would construe as an ominously nationalistic and aggressively aroused China.

Since the United States has been militarily deployed on the basis of treaty commitments in Japan and South Korea for several decades, how Beijing conducts itself in its immediate neighborhood will impact directly the overall American-Chinese relationship. Broadly speaking, the current strategic goals of the rising but still cautiously deliberate China appear to be driven by the following six major objectives:

1. To reduce the dangers inherent in China's potential geographical encirclement, due to: the US security links with Japan, South Korea, and the Philippines; the vulnerability to interdiction of China's maritime access into the Indian Ocean through the Strait of Malacca and thence to the Middle East, Africa, Europe, and so on; and the absence of available economically sustainable land routes for trade with Europe through the vast distances of Russia and/or Central Asia;
2. To establish for itself a favored position in an emerging East Asian community (which could include a China-Japan-South Korea free trade zone) and likewise in the already-existing ASEAN, while containing—though not yet excluding—a major US presence or role in them;
3. To consolidate Pakistan as a counterweight to India and to gain through it a more proximate and safer access to the Arabian Sea and the Persian Gulf;
4. To gain a significant edge over Russia in economic influence in Central Asia and Mongolia, thereby satisfying in part China's needs for natural resources also in areas closer to China than Africa or Latin America;

5. To resolve in China's favor the remaining unsettled legacy of its civil war—Taiwan—in keeping with Deng's formula (first enunciated publicly to the Chinese media in the course of a visit to him by this writer) of "one China, two systems"; and
6. To establish for itself a favored economic, and indirectly political, presence in a number of Middle Eastern, African, and Latin American countries, thereby securing stable access to raw materials, minerals, agricultural products, and energy—while simultaneously securing a dominant position in local markets for China's competitively priced manufactured products, and, in the process, thereby gaining a global political constituency on China's behalf.

The aforementioned six major strategic goals are a mixture of the country's geopolitical and economic interests in what some Chinese strategists have described as China's "Grand Periphery," but they also reflect China's historical view of its rightful entitlement to a dominant regional—perhaps eventually global—role. They are not rooted, as was the case with the Soviet Union, in universal ideological aspirations. But they do reflect Chinese pride and presumed desire, disguised for the time being, for China to become again—as it once was—the world's preeminent power, even replacing America. Indeed, it is already noticeable that China's intelligently calculated foreign outreach—built around slogans regarding "a harmonious world"—is beginning to intrigue the political imagination of peoples in the world's less privileged parts. For the many who crave a vision of a more relevant future than offered by the "waning American dream," China is beginning to offer a new option, that of the rising Chinese dream.

Each of the six Chinese goals can be sought flexibly and patiently, or China can pursue each goal aggressively, in order to undermine America's position in the East. For example, Japan and South Korea can be partners in an East Asian community that accepts America's involvement in it, or they can be enticed into one with a united Korea under a Chinese umbrella and a neutral Japan detached from the United States (similarly with the other examples). In essence, the intensity of Chinese nationalism is likely to determine whether the above goals can be assimilated into a pattern of accommodation, largely with the United States, or whether they become objectives to be sought assertively, by a nationalistically aroused China increasingly preoccupied with an antagonistic contestation with the United States.

Which of these two becomes more likely will depend on two fundamental considerations: how America will respond to an ascending China, and how China itself will evolve. The acumen and maturity of both nations are likely to be severely tested in the process, and the stakes for each will be enormous. For America, therefore, the task is to disentangle which aspects of China's external ambitions are unacceptable and pose a direct threat to vital American interests, and which aspects reflect new historical geopolitical and economic realities that can be accommodated, however reluctantly, without damage to key US interests. In effect, to assess calmly what is not worth a collision with China and where the lines should be drawn so that China itself realizes that going beyond would prove counterproductive to its own interests and/or beyond its means to assert. The ultimate goal, but not at any price, should be a China that is a constructive and major partner in world affairs.

It follows that in seeking to increase the probability that China becomes a major global partner, America should tacitly accept the reality of China's geopolitical preeminence on the mainland of Asia, as well as China's ongoing emergence as the predominant Asian economic power. But the prospects of a comprehensive American-Chinese global partnership will actually be enhanced if America at the same time retains a significant geopolitical presence of its own in the Far East, based on its continued ties with Japan, South Korea, the Philippines, Singapore, and Indonesia—and does so whether China approves or not. Such a presence would encourage in general the Asian neighbors of China (including also those not explicitly mentioned) to take advantage of America's involvement in Asia's financial and economic structures—as well as of America's geopolitical presence—to pursue peacefully but with greater self-confidence their own independence and interests in the shadow of a powerful China.

Japan is a crucial ally for the United States in its effort to develop a stable American-Chinese partnership. Its ties with America underline the fact that America is a Pacific Ocean power, just as America's ties with Great Britain confirm the reality of America being also an Atlantic Ocean power. Both sets of ties make possible America's variable partnerships with Europe and China respectively. Progressive and deepening reconciliation between China and Japan is, in the above context, also a major American interest. The American presence in Japan, and especially the security links between the two countries, should facilitate such a reconciliation. That would be especially so if it is sought in the context of a serious effort by America and China to deepen and expand the scope of their own bilateral cooperation.

At the same time, an internationally more active and militarily more capable Japan would also be a more positive contributor to global stability. Some prominent Japanese have even been urging that Japan joins the nascent Trans-Pacific Partnership (TPP), favored by the United States, which aims at free trade between the states located on the rim of the Pacific Ocean (and denounced by Chinese experts as a plot against the East Asian community). Japan would still lack the power to threaten China, but it could contribute more to international peace enforcement and generally act more in keeping with its significant economic status. Issues between it and China pertaining to the potentially oil-rich islands claimed by both of them could then be resolved more easily by following established procedures for international mediation and adjudication.

South Korea, as long as it remains potentially threatened and with the peninsula divided, has no choice but to depend on America's security commitments—with those in turn dependent for their effectiveness on America's continued presence in Japan. Despite extensive trade relations, the historic enmity between Korea and Japan has so far prevented any close military cooperation even though it is in the evident security interest of both. The more secure South Korea is, the less likely there is to be some unexpected assault from the North. Eventually, the issue of peaceful reunification may become timely, and at that moment China's role may be crucial in facilitating perhaps a reunification by stages. Should that happen, the South Koreans may decide to reassess the degree to which some reduction in their security ties with the United States and especially with Japan might become acceptable as a trade-off for Chinese-assisted national reunification.

Closer US political and commercial ties with Indonesia, Singapore, Malaysia, Vietnam, and the maintenance of the historical US connection with the Philippines would also enhance the prospects for Asian support for direct US participation in the expanding architecture of regional interstate cooperation. The interests of each of these states in such a relationship with the United States would also have the effect of generating greater Chinese understanding that America's Pacific Ocean strategy is not meant to contain China but rather to engage it in a larger web of cooperative relationships that indirectly will also help to shape the bilateral US-Chinese global partnership.

In that larger context of economic and political cooperation, three sensitive US-Chinese issues will have to be peacefully resolved, the first of them probably in the near future, the second in the course of the next several years, and the third within a decade or so, assuming continued constructive development of the bilateral American-Chinese relationship within wider Asian regional cooperation.

The first of these sensitive issues pertains to the American reconnaissance operations on the edges of Chinese territorial waters (six miles from shore) as well as periodic American naval patrols within international waters that also happen to be part of the Chinese economic zone. These activities understandably are provocative to the Chinese, and there is little doubt that the American public would be aroused if China was to reciprocate in kind. Moreover, the air reconnaissance poses serious risks of unintentional collisions, since the Chinese usually respond to such US air reconnaissance by sending up their fighter planes for up-close inspection and perhaps even harassment.

Some accommodation regarding the foregoing could be furthered by addressing on a more systematic basis the second increasingly contentious issue, namely the relationship between the military buildups undertaken by both states. The American defense budget and the scale of the American arms program are infinitely larger, in part because America is engaged currently in warfare and in part because of its global commitments. At this stage, China's response is primarily regional, but it does directly affect American security concerns as well as America's commitments to its Asian allies. A systematic effort by the two states, therefore, to reach some sort of agreement regarding longer-range military plans and measures of reciprocal reassurance is certainly a necessary component of any longer-term US-Chinese partnership as well as a source of reassurance to Japan and South Korea. The absence of any such accommodation will almost inevitably become an insurmountable obstacle, gradually not only undermining the existing cooperation but also potentially creating a serious arms race.

The third long-term geopolitical problem is ultimately the most difficult, but its resolution could be facilitated by progress in regard to the aforementioned first two. It pertains to the future status of Taiwan. The United States no longer recognizes Taiwan as a sovereign state and acknowledges the Chinese view that China and Taiwan are part of a single nation. A long-term US-Chinese accommodation at some point will have to address the fact that a separate Taiwan cannot be protected by American arms sales without provoking Chinese enmity, and that a Chinese-type resolution along the lines of Deng Xiaoping's longstanding formula of "one China, two systems," provides an elastic formula for both unification and yet distinct political, social, and even separate military arrangements. (Hence it should be redefined as "one China, several systems.")

The "one China, two systems" formula, in its narrower form, has been tested in Hong Kong since the extension of Chinese sovereignty to that former British colony. Its internal autonomy, including democracy, has proven viable even though the PLA (the Chinese army) has been deployed there. And given China's growing status, it is doubtful that Taiwan can reject indefinitely its inclusion in China on the basis of a more flexible interpretation of the "one China, several systems" formula, therefore not including a PLA presence on the island. Obviously, the willingness of China and America to reach an accommodation on this politically and morally sensitive issue will depend on the nature of the overall relationship between the two countries. The resolution of the first two issues would eliminate the most likely sources of geopolitical hostility in the near term. In the longer run, failure to address the third one could produce a truly serious rupture in the relationship, especially since the United States conceded already under President Nixon its acceptance of the principle shared by both China and Taiwan that there is only one China.

Ultimately, as noted earlier, a great deal will depend also on the internal condition of both countries. An America that renews its infrastructure, that reenergizes its technological innovation, that regains its sense of historical optimism, and that overcomes its paralyzing political gridlock will be an America that can more confidently adjust to, and cope with, a rising China. Such an America will be likely to have a clearer, less Manichean view of the world, and thus would be better able to face a world in which its political preeminence has to be in some degree shared.

Likewise, much depends on how China continues to evolve. Its last two hundred years have been turbulent and disruptive. Its contemporary stability and progress are only thirty years old. Its nineteenth century was onc of disruption, decay, and violent foreign military interventions as well as humiliating foreign "concessions." Its twentieth century was one of almost continuous strife in the context of national awakening. Sun Yat-sen and later Chiang Kai-shek were China's failed equivalents of Turkey's successful Ataturk. Mao Zedong was a self-destructive equivalent of Russia's equally brutal Stalin. Only Deng Xiaoping accomplished what Gorbachev failed to do in the Soviet Union: to set China on a so-far-successful course of domestic transformation by tapping simultaneously the personal aspirations of the Chinese people as well as their aroused national ambitions.

Assuming continued domestic success, it is unlikely that China will experience in the relatively near future—say by 2030—what many in the West hope: the emergence of a middle-class-based constitutional democracy of the American-European variety. (Note that it took Taiwan approximately sixty years to evolve—with sympathetic and influential US encouragement—from authoritarianism to constitutional democracy.) Retaining national unity in the context of modernity—increasing access to the outside world, expanding interactions via the Internet, and rising but unequal standards of living—is thus more likely to involve two basic alternatives, but with neither being an imitation of a multiparty Western-type pluralist democracy. The dangerous one has already been discussed: a modernizing China that is assertive, impatient, triumphalist, and aggressively nationalistic in which the PLA is the source of authority and action. Such a China would endanger not only the outside world, but also itself.

A less internationally troubling alternative to a nationalistic China motivated by twentieth-century European-style chauvinism could be the emergence of what might be called a Confucian China with modern characteristics. China's political culture has deep roots, and it is suffused with its own distinctive philosophical concepts of life, of hierarchy, and of authority. The notion of domestic "harmony," in which unity asserted by an authoritarian framework is said to originate from a generalized philosophical consensus, in which leadership emerges through meritocratic selection but not open political contestation, and in which policy is derived from "facts" but is not dogmatized is deeply rooted in China's long past. It is noteworthy that Deng Xiaoping repeatedly cited the phrase "seek truth from facts," pointedly echoing Confucius.

China's leadership is also profoundly conscious of the "fact" that its vast numbers of increasingly elderly citizens will be imposing greater strains on social cohesion—thus threatening the Confucian notion of "harmony." (President Jiang Zemin was once asked by this author what his main domestic problem was, and he instantly replied with just three words: "Too many Chinese.") Chinese officials have also publicly acknowledged the growing risks inherent in their country's increasingly evident social disparities and in the persisting reality of hundreds of millions of Chinese still not benefiting from China's ongoing transformation. That, too, makes coping with these domestic risks to internal "harmony" more important than projecting a universal doctrine.

In any case, the notion of harmony is the message that China is increasingly and deliberately attempting to convey about itself to the world at large. Ruled by an officialdom that calls itself the Communist Party, China in its global outreach does not identify itself with the class struggle nor with an eventual world revolution (on the Soviet mode) but relates itself more to its Confucian past and its Buddhist roots. Symptomatically, China's main vehicle for an international dialogue about itself are the several hundred Confucius Institutes actively being established around the world, modeled on the French Alliance Française and the UK's British Councils. In addition to acquainting outsiders with Confucius' teachings, China's Buddhist heritage (shared with its neighbors) is now also publicly acknowledged. That message, as a practical matter, does not offer much guidance regarding China's global intentions and strategy. But its emphasis on "peaceful rising" and global harmony does allow at least for a dialogue and for China's comprehensive integration into the international system.

In that setting and in the longer run, it is doubtful that China could make itself permanently impermeable to pressures from an increasingly interdependent and interconnected world from which it could perhaps only isolate itself at great cost. The cumulative consequences of the emergence of an internationally aware middle class, the countless Chinese who will have studied abroad, the inevitably growing appeal to millions of university students of democracy as a way of life as well as the expression of their personal dignity, the sheer inability in the age of interactive communications of even a determined political elite to impose on society airtight ideological isolation, all argue for the proposition that an eventually modern and more prosperous China, too, will become more inclined to join the democratic mainstream.

The fact that by 2050 China will be a relatively middle-aged society, somewhat like today's Japan—currently 22% of the latter's population is aged sixty-five or older, and projections indicate that by midcentury so will be 25% of China's—also justifies the hypothesis that such a change may not come as abruptly as in the case of societies with potentially explosive demographic youth bulges. Indeed, the changing demographic profile of a more middle-aged as well as middle-class China is likely to facilitate a more evolutionary adoption of political pluralism as a normal progression toward a more refined political culture, compatible with China's traditions.

In that evolving historical context, America's geopolitical role in the new East will have to be fundamentally different from its direct involvement in the renewal of the West. There, America is the essential source of the needed stimulus for geopolitical renovation and even territorial outreach. In Asia, an America cooperatively engaged in multilateral structures, cautiously supportive of India's development, solidly tied to Japan and South Korea, and patiently expanding both bilateral as well as global cooperation with China is the best source of the balancing leverage needed for sustaining stability in the globally rising new East.

- CONCLUSION -

America's Dual Role

DURING THE FIRST HALF OF THE FIRST MILLENNIUM—MORE THAN 1,500 years ago—the politics of the relatively civilized parts of Europe were largely dominated by the coexistence of the two distinct western and eastern halves of the Roman Empire. The western empire, with its capital most of the time in Rome, was beset by conflicts with marauding barbarians. With its troops permanently stationed abroad in extensive and expensive fortifications, the politically overextended Rome came close to bankrupting itself midway through the fifth century. Simultaneously, divisive conflicts between Christians and pagans sapped its social cohesion and heavy taxation and corruption crippled its economic vitality. In AD 476, with the fall of Romulus Augustus to the barbarians, the by-then moribund western Roman Empire officially collapsed. During the same period, the eastern Roman Empire—soon to become known as Byzantium—displayed more dynamism in its urbanization and economic growth while proving to be more successful in its diplomatic and security policies. After the fall of Rome, Byzantium continued to thrive for centuries. It reconquered parts of the old western empire and lived on—though later through much conflict—until the rise of the Ottoman Turks in the fifteenth century.

The importance of this historical diversion is as a point of contrast to the dynamics of the world in the twenty-first century. Rome's dire travails in the middle of the fifth century did not damage Byzantium's more hopeful prospects, because in those days the world was compartmentalized into distinct segments geographically isolated and politically and economically insulated from one another. The fate of one did not directly and immediately affect the prospects of the other. Today, with distance made irrelevant by rapid communications and instant financial transactions, the well-being of the economically, financially, and militarily most advanced parts of the world is becoming increasingly interdependent. In our time, unlike 1,500 years ago, the organic relationship between the West and the East can be either reciprocally cooperative or mutually damaging.

Thus, America's central challenge and its geopolitically imperative mission over the next several decades is to revitalize itself and to promote a larger and more vital West while simultaneously buttressing a complex balance in the East, so as to accommodate constructively China's rising global status and avert global chaos. Without a stable geopolitical balance in Eurasia promoted by a renewed America, progress on the issues of central importance to social well-being and ultimately to human survival would stall. America's failure to pursue an ambitious transcontinental geopolitical vision would likely accelerate the decline of the West and prompt more instability in the East. In Asia, national rivalries, foremost between China and India and Japan, would contribute to greater regional tensions while eventually intensifying the latent hostility between China and America, to the detriment of both.

Alternatively, a successful American effort to enlarge the West, making it the world's most stable and also most democratic zone, would seek to combine power with principle. A cooperative larger West, extending from North America through Europe into Eurasia and embracing Russia as well as Turkey, would geographically reach Japan, the first Asian state to embrace democracy successfully, as well as South Korea. That wider outreach would enhance the appeal of its core principles to other cultures, and thus encourage the gradual emergence in the decades ahead of varied forms of a universal democratic political culture.

At the same time, America should continue to engage cooperatively in the energetic and financially influential but also potentially conflicted East. If America and China can accommodate each other on a broad range of issues, the prospects for stability in Asia will be greatly increased. That is likely to be the case especially if the United States can at the same time encourage a genuine reconciliation between Japan—its principal Pacific Ocean ally—and China, as well as mitigate the growing rivalry between China and India. These concurrent goals are important because one should not lose sight of the fact that Asia is much more than China. US policy in the East has to take into account that the quest for a stable Asian equilibrium cannot be confined to a China-centric concentration on a special partnership with Beijing, desirable as that is.

Hence to respond effectively in both the western and eastern parts of Eurasia, America must adopt a dual role. It must be the *promoter* and *guarantor* of greater and broader unity in the West, and it must be the *balancer* and *conciliator* between the major powers in the East. Both roles are essential and each is needed to reinforce the other. But to have the credibility and the capacity to pursue both successfully, America needs to show the world that it has the will to renovate itself at home. Leaving aside the increasingly questionable statistical presumption that current national rates of growth will continue indefinitely for decades, Americans must place greater emphasis on other dimensions of national power such as innovation, education, the ability to balance intelligently force and diplomacy, the quality of political leadership, and the attraction of a democratic life-style.

For America to succeed as the promoter and guarantor of a renewed West, close American-European ties, a continuing US commitment to NATO, and careful American-European management of a step-by-step process of embracing, perhaps in varying ways, both Turkey and a truly democratizing Russia into the West will be essential. The United States must encourage the deeper unification of the European Union and guarantee its geopolitical relevance by remaining active in

European security, while pushing Europe to increase its own political and military activity. The close cooperation between Britain, France, and Germany—Europe's central political, economic, and military alignment—should continue and broaden. Additionally, the expanding German-French-Polish consultations regarding Europe's eastern policy—critical to the EU's eastern accommodation and expansion—must simultaneously strengthen and expand. America is the critical source of historical stimulus for this project because without its active presence the new and still fragile European unity could fragment.

In strategically engaging Russia while safeguarding Western unity, the French-German-Polish "Weimar triangle" can play a constructive role in advancing and consolidating the ongoing but still tenuous reconciliation between Poland and Russia. Franco-German support for this reconciliation would both enhance Poland's sense of security and reassure Russia that the process has a larger European dimension. Only then might the much desirable Russian-Polish reconciliation become truly comprehensive, as the German-Polish one has already become, and both reconciliations would then contribute to greater stability in Europe. But in order for the Polish-Russian reconciliation to be productive and enduring, it has to move from the governmental level to the social level, through extensive people-to-people contacts and numerous joint educational initiatives. Expedient accommodations by governments, not grounded in basic changes in popular attitudes, will not last. In 1939, Hitler's Nazi regime in Germany and Stalin's regime in Soviet Russia made such a grand accommodation, yet two years later they were at war.

In contrast, the post–World War II Franco-German friendship, while initiated at the highest levels (with both General de Gaulle and Chancellor Adenauer playing historical roles), was also successfully promoted on the social and cultural level. Even respective French and German national narratives have become fundamentally compatible, providing a solid base for genuinely good neighborly relations—and thus a firm foundation for a peaceful alliance. Exactly the same process needs repetition in the Polish-Russian case, and once it gains momentum it will generate its own positive international effects. Poland, moreover, could then play not only a critical role in opening the doors of Europe to Russia but also in encouraging Ukraine and Belarus to move in the same direction on their own, thus increasing Russia's interests in doing likewise. The desirable historical process of enlarging the West thus has to be strategically guided and solidly grounded. It must be backed by a larger Atlantic alliance within which Poland genuinely partners with a Germany that in turn is linked in friendship closely to France.

The foregoing will require both America's and Europe's persistence and strategic scrutiny. And Russia itself will have to evolve in order to meet EU standards. But in the long run, Russia will not want to be left out of this opportunity, especially if Turkey and the EU make progress in resolving current obstacles. Moreover, a significant portion of Russia's public is ahead of its government regarding EU membership. A poll conducted in Russia in early 2011 by Deutsche Welle, the German international broadcasting service, indicated that 23% of Russians feel that Russia should become a member of the EU in the course of the next two years, 16% in two to five years, 9% in five to ten years, 6% much longer, while 28% were not sure and only 18% were flatly against. But while they favor EU membership, the Russian public is generally unaware of the exacting character of the qualifying standards for EU membership. At best, as is already the case with Turkey, the process of admission is likely to move forward, then stall, and lurch forward again, probably by stages and perhaps through transitional arrangements. At this time, however, it would be premature to attempt to draw a detailed blueprint for the exact political architecture of an eventually enlarged West.

However, if America does not promote the emergence of a more unified West, dire consequences could follow. European historical resentments could reawaken, new conflicts of interest could arise, and shortsighted competitive partnerships could take shape. Russia could divisively exploit its energy assets and, emboldened by Western disunity, seek to absorb Ukraine quickly, reawakening its own imperial ambitions and contributing to greater international disarray. With Europe passive, individual European states, in search of greater commercial opportunities, could then seek accommodation with Russia. One can envisage a scenario in which a special relationship develops between Russia and Germany or Italy because of economic self-interest. The UK would then become closer to the United States in a negative reaction to a crumbling and politically contentious union. France and Britain would also draw closer together while viewing Germany askance, with Poland and the Baltic states desperately pleading for additional US security guarantees. The result would not be a new and more vital West, but rather a progressively splintering West with its vision shrinking.

Moreover, such a disunited West could not compete confidently with China for global systemic relevance. So far, China has not articulated an ideological dogma that claims its recent performance is globally applicable and the United States has been careful not to make ideology the central focus of its relations with key countries, recognizing that compromises on other issues are sometimes unavoidable (as for example, arms control with Russia). Wisely, both the United States and China have explicitly embraced the concept of "a constructive partnership" in global affairs, and the United States—while critical of China's violations of human rights—has been careful not to stigmatize the Chinese socioeconomic system as a whole. But even in such a less antagonistic setting, a larger and renewed West would be in a much better position to compete peacefully—and without ideological fervor—with China as to which system is a better model for the developing world in its efforts to address the aspirations of its now politically awakened masses.

But if an anxious America and an overconfident China were to slide into increasing political hostility, it is more than likely that both countries would face off in a mutually destructive ideological conflict. America would argue that China's success is based on tyranny and is damaging to America's economic well-being. The Chinese would interpret that American message as an attempt to undermine and possibly even to fragment the Chinese system. At the same time, China increasingly would represent itself to the world as a rejection of Western supremacy, connecting it with the era of rapacious exploitation of the weak by the strong, appealing ideologically to those in the third world who already subscribe to a historical narrative highly hostile to the West in general and lately to America in particular. It follows that both America and China, out of intelligent self-interest, would be better served by mutual ideological self-restraint. Both should resist the temptation to universalize the distinctive features of their respective socio-economic systems and to demonize each other.

In regard to the longer-term issue of Asian stability, the United States must play the role of balancer and conciliator. It should therefore avoid direct military involvement in Asia and it should seek to reconcile the long-standing animosities between key Far Eastern Asian players, most notably between China and Japan. In the new East, the cardinal principle guiding US policy has to be that the United States will engage on the mainland of Asia in response to hostile actions only if directed at states in which treaty-based American deployments are part of the long-standing international context.

In essence, America's engagement in Asia as the balancer of regional stability should replicate the role played by Great Britain in intra-European politics during the nineteenth and early twentieth centuries. The United States can and should be the key player in helping Asia avoid a struggle for regional domination, by mediating conflicts and offsetting power imbalances among potential rivals. In doing so, it should respect China's special historical and geopolitical role in maintaining stability on the Far Eastern mainland. Engaging with China in a serious dialogue regarding regional stability would not only help reduce the possibility of American-Chinese conflicts but also diminish the probability of miscalculation between China and Japan, or China and India, and even at some point between China and Russia over the resources and status of the Central Asian states. Thus, America's balancing engagement in Asia is ultimately in China's interest as well.

At the same time, the United States must recognize that stability in Asia can no longer be imposed by a non-Asian power, least of all (especially after the inconclusive Korean War, the failed Vietnamese War, the unprovoked attack on Iraq in 2003, and the prolonged Afghan conflict) by the direct application of US military power. Indeed, US efforts to enhance Asian stability could prove self-defeating—propelling the United States into a costly repeat of its recent wars—and even result in a replay of what transpired in Europe during the twentieth century. If America became active in fashioning an anti-Chinese alliance with India (and perhaps with some other mainland states) or in promoting an anti-Chinese militarization of Japan, it could generate dangerous mutual resentment. Geopolitical equilibrium in twenty-first-century Asia has to be based more on a regionally self-sustaining and constructive approach to interstate relations and less on regionally divisive military alliances with non-Asian powers.

Accordingly, the guiding principle of America's policy as a balancer and conciliator in the East must be the notion that, save for its obligations to Japan and Korea, America should not allow itself to be drawn into a war between Asian powers on the mainland. The reality is that while such wars would be debilitating to the protagonists, vital American interests would not be threatened by them. But in relation to Japan and Korea, the United States has been entrenched in these two countries for more than fifty years as the result of World War II. The independence and the self-confidence of these countries would be shattered—along with America's role in the Pacific—if any doubts arose regarding the durability of long-standing American treaty-based commitments. Moreover, Japan is an offshore island and in that respect its relationship with America—as America's principal ally in the Far East—is somewhat reminiscent of America's ties with Great Britain, particularly during World War II and the uncertain years of the Cold War. South Korea, currently divided, is an extension of that relationship and the United States would place its own long-term interests in the Far East in jeopardy if the seriousness of its commitment to the defense of these two countries became unreliable. However, America can play a constructive role in promoting restraint between the key players—and therefore avoid the cost of a war to protect Japan or Korea—through active political, diplomatic, and economic support for a regional balance of power. Doing so would both enhance America's political influence and contribute to greater Asian stability.

America's role as conciliator in the East will be especially critical, particularly in regard to the relationship between Japan and China. The American-Japanese relationship, and through it the promotion of a Chinese-Japanese reconciliation, should be the springboard for a concerted effort to develop an American-Japanese-Chinese cooperative triangle. Such a triangle would provide the structure to deal with strategic concerns resulting from China's increased regional presence on a constructive basis. Just as stability in Europe would not have developed without progressive expansion of the Franco-German reconciliation to the German-Polish reconciliation, which in turn has facilitated the emergence of a tacit German-French-Polish security coordination, so the deliberate nurturing of a deepening Chinese-Japanese relationship—especially also on a social and cultural level—can likewise be the point of departure for greater stability in the Far East.

In the context of this triangular relationship, Chinese-Japanese reconciliation would help to enhance and to solidify a more comprehensive American-Chinese cooperation. The Chinese know that America's commitment to Japan is steadfast, that the bond between the two is deep and genuine, and that Japan's security is directly dependent on America. And the Japanese know that a conflict with China would be reciprocally destructive and hence American engagement with China is indirectly a contribution to Japan's security and well-being. Given this dynamic, China would not view American support for Japan's security as a threat, and nor would Japan view the pursuit of a closer and globally more extensive American-Chinese partnership, verging in effect on a very informal geopolitical G-2 arrangement, as a threat to its own interests. A deepening triangular relationship could also diminish Japanese concerns over the eventual elevation of the renminbi to the status of the world's third currency, thereby further consolidating China's stake in the existing international system and thus mitigating American anxieties over China's future role.

In brief, an active American role in Asia is essential not only in order to promote stability in the region but, even more so, to create circumstances in which the American-Chinese relationship evolves peacefully and cooperatively, and eventually grows into a wide-ranging political and economic global partnership. Indeed, the relationship between America and China may well become the crucible of the ability of the world's most populated and economically most dynamic Eurasian continent to blend domestic success with regional stability.

Historically, America has shown that it rises to the occasion when challenged. But the world of the twenty-first century presents far different challenges than those in the past. The world is now almost everywhere politically awakened—with millions stirring restlessly in pursuit of a better future. It is also experiencing the dispersal of global power—with several new aspirants rapidly rising in the East. Consequently, today's world is much less susceptible to domination by a single power, even by one as militarily powerful and politically influential as the United States. But, since America is not yet Rome and China is not yet its Byzantium, a stable global order ultimately depends on America's ability to renew itself and to act wisely as the *promoter* and *guarantor* of a revitalized West and as the *balancer* and *conciliator* of a rising new East.

AFTERWORD TO THE PAPERBACK EDITION

Applying Strategic Vision to Some Current as Well as Emerging Dilemmas

SINCE WRITING THIS BOOK, THREE ISSUES HAVE BECOME increasingly important, urgent, and perhaps even dangerous. The first involves the rising tensions in the Middle East, where stability is threatened by a confluence of events in Iran, Israel, and Syria, and where the threat of war looms particularly large between Israel and Iran. Second is the future of long-run stability in Asia, and in particular the role in that regard of the US-China relationship. The final issue pertains to the rising possibility of what are in effect invisible wars—pursued via cyber attacks, drone strikes, and transnational terror networks by unknown sources. How America handles these specific challenges will be critical to its overall prospects beyond 2020 and unto 2050.*

* The views expressed here initially appeared in three of my op-eds: "The 'Stupidest' War? Iran Should Be Key Topic at Hearings," *Washington Post* (1/3/2013); "Giants, but Not Hegemons," *New York Times/International Herald Tribune* (2/13/2013); and "The Cyber Age Demands New Rules of War," *Financial Times* (2/24/2013). They have been amended to fit this essay.

On Iran

Determining how to deal with Iran's nuclear program is perhaps the most immediate challenge facing the United States. An offensive strike on Iran, as some desire, would be a colossal mistake. It is essential therefore that the issue of war or peace with Iran be fully vented, specifically with the US national interest foremost in mind. Although the President has skillfully avoided a specific commitment to military action by a certain date, the absence of a negotiated agreement with Iran regarding its compliance with the Nuclear Nonproliferation Treaty will inevitably intensify some foreign and extremist domestic clamor for US military action, alone or in coordination with Israel.

Accordingly, five potential implications for the United States of a self-generated war deserve close scrutiny:

- How effective are US military strikes against Iranian nuclear facilities likely to be, with consequences of what duration and at what human cost to the Iranian people?
- What might be Iran's retaliatory responses against US interests, and with what consequences for regional stability? How damaging could resulting instability be to European and Asian economies?
- Could a US attack be justified as in keeping with international standards, and would the UN Security Council—particularly China and Russia, given their veto power—be likely to endorse it?
- Since Israel is considered to have more than 100 nuclear weapons, how credible is the argument that Iran might attack Israel without first itself acquiring a significant nuclear arsenal, including a survivable second-strike capability—prospects that are at least some years away?
- Could some alternative US strategic commitment provide a more enduring and less reckless arrangement for neutralizing the potential Iranian nuclear threat than a unilateral initiation of war in a combustible regional setting?

Best available estimates suggest that a limited US strike would have only a temporary effect. Repetitive attacks would be more effective, but civilian fatalities would rise accordingly, and there would be ghastly risks of released radiation. Iranian nationalism would be galvanized into prolonged hatred of the United States, to the political benefit of the ruling regime.

Iran, in retaliating, could make life more difficult for US forces in western Afghanistan by activating a new guerrilla front. Tehran could also precipitate explosive violence in Iraq, which in turn could set the entire region on fire, with conflicts spreading through Syria to Lebanon and even Jordan. Although the US Navy should be able to keep the Strait of Hormuz open, escalating insurance costs for the flow of oil would adversely affect the economies of Europe and Asia. The United States would be widely blamed.

Given the recently woeful US performance in the United Nations—where the United States and Israel gained the support of only 7 states out of 188 in opposing UN membership for Palestine—it is also safe to predict that an unsanctioned US attack on Iran would create worldwide outrage. Might the UN General Assembly then condemn the United States? The result would be unprecedented international isolation for an America already deeply embroiled in the region's protracted turmoil.

Congress should also take note that our Middle Eastern and European friends who advocate US military action against Iran are usually quite reticent to shed their own blood in a new Middle East conflict. To make matters worse, the most immediate beneficiary of an ill-considered recourse to war would be Vladimir Putin's Russia, which would be able to charge Europe almost at will for its oil while gaining a free hand to threaten Georgia and Azerbaijan and thus cut off Europe's access to Caspian energy sources.

It follows therefore that a failure to reach a satisfactory negotiated solution with Iran should not be viewed as the trigger for a new US-initiated war that is not likely to be confined to Iran. A more prudent and productive course for the United States would be to continue the painful sanctions against Iran while formally adopting for the Middle East the same policy that for decades successfully protected America's European and Asian allies against the much more dangerous threats emanating from Stalinist Russia and, lately, from nuclear-armed North Korea. The United States would make a public commitment that an Iranian military threat aimed at Israel or any other US friend in the Middle East would be treated as if directed at the United States itself and would precipitate a commensurate US response.

A serious public discussion of these issues may help generate a firmer national consensus that a reckless shortcut to war—which is favored now by neither the American people nor the Israeli public—is not the wisest response to a potentially grave crisis. Indeed, could Meir Dagan, the former head of Israel's Mossad, have been right when he bluntly said that an attack on Iran is "the stupidest thing I have ever heard"? Fortunately, there is a better, even if not a perfect, option.

On Asian Conflicts

Though its tensions are the most acute, the Middle East is not the only point of global contention; the risk of regional conflicts also exists in Asia. In the long run, maintaining a successful relationship between the United States and China will be even more decisive in preventing the escalation of tension in the region, even though many fear that the emerging American-Chinese duopoly must inevitably lead to conflict. Admittedly, the historical record is dismal. Since the onset of global politics 200 years ago, four long wars (including the Cold War) were fought over the domination of Europe, each of which could have resulted in global hegemony by a sole superpower.

Yet several developments over recent years have changed the equation. Nuclear weapons make hegemonic wars too destructive, and thus render victory meaningless. One-sided national economic triumphs cannot be achieved in the increasingly interwoven global economy without precipitating calamitous consequences for everyone. Further, the populations of the world are now largely awakened politically and thus are not so easily subdued, even by the most powerful. Last but not least, neither the United States nor China is driven by hostile ideologies.

Moreover, despite our very different political systems, both our societies are, in different ways, open. That, too, offsets pressure from within each respective society toward animus and hostility. More than 100,000 Chinese are students at American universities, and thousands of young Americans study and work in China or participate in special study or travel programs. Unlike in the former Soviet Union, millions of Chinese regularly travel abroad. Last year, some 1.3 million Chinese visitors came to the United States and millions of young Chinese are in daily touch with the world through the Internet.

All this contrasts greatly with the societal self-isolation of the nineteenth- and twentieth-century contestants for global power, which intensified grievances, escalated hostility, and made it easier to demonize one another. Nonetheless, we cannot entirely ignore the fact that the hopeful expectation in recent years of an amicable American-Chinese relationship has lately been tested by ever-more antagonistic polemics, especially in the mass media of both sides. This has been fueled in part by speculation about America's allegedly inevitable decline and about China's relentless, rapid rise.

Pessimism about America's future tends to underestimate its capacity for self-renewal. Exuberant optimists about China's inevitable preeminence underestimate the gap that still separates China from America—whether in terms of GDP per capita or respective technological capabilities. Paradoxically, China's truly admirable economic success is now intensifying the systemic need for complex social and political adjustments in how and to what extent a ruling bureaucracy that defines itself as communist can continue to direct a system of state capitalism with a rising middle class that seeks more rights.

Simplistic agitation regarding the potential Chinese military threat to America ignores the advantages that the United States also derives from its very favorable geostrategic location on the open shores of two great oceans as well as from its transoceanic allies on all sides. In contrast, China is geographically encircled by not-always-friendly states and has very few, if any, allies. On occasion, some of China's neighbors are tempted by this circumstance to draw the United States into support of their specific claims against, or conflicts of interest with, China. Fortunately, there are signs that a consensus is emerging that such threats should not be resolved unilaterally or militarily, but through negotiation.

Matters have not been helped by the American media's characterization of the Obama administration's relative rebalancing of focus toward Asia as a "pivot" (though the word was never used by the President himself) with military connotations. In fact, the renewed focus on Asia was only meant to be a constructive reaffirmation of the unchanged reality that the United States is both a Pacific and an Atlantic power.

Taking all this into account, the real threat to a stable US-China relationship does not arise from any hostile intentions on the part of either country, but from the disturbing possibility that a revitalized Asia may slide into the kind of nationalistic fervor that precipitated conflicts in twentieth-century Europe over resources, territory, or power. There are plenty of potential flash points: North Korea versus South Korea, China versus Japan, China versus India, or India versus Pakistan. The danger is that if governments incite or allow nationalistic fervor as a kind of safety valve, the nationalist sentiment can spin out of control.

In such a potentially explosive context, US political and economic involvement in Asia can be a crucially needed stabilizing factor. Indeed, America's current role in Asia should be analogous to Britain's role in nineteenth-century Europe as an "offshore" balancing influence with no entanglements in the region's rivalries and no attempt to attain domination over the region. To be effective, constructive, and strategically sensitive, US engagement in Asia must not be based solely on existing alliances with Japan and South Korea. Engagement must also mean institutionalizing US-Chinese cooperation.

Accordingly, America and China should deliberately prevent their economic competition from turning into political hostility. Bilateral and multilateral mutual engagement—and not reciprocal exclusion—is what is needed. For example, the United States ought not to seek a "trans-Pacific partnership" without China, and China should not seek a Regional Comprehensive Economic Pact without the United States. History can avoid repeating the calamitous conflicts of the twentieth century if America is present in Asia as a stabilizer—not a would-be policeman—and if China becomes the preeminent, but not domineering, power in the region.

In January 2011, President Obama and recently retired Chinese President Hu Jintao met and issued a communiqué boldly detailing joint undertakings and proposing to build a historically unprecedented partnership between America and China. With Obama's reelection in 2012 and Xi Jinping's assumption of China's presidency in March 2013, the two leaders should meet regularly to revalidate and reenergize the US-China relationship. Whether this relationship is either vital and robust or weak and full of suspicion will affect the whole world.

On Anonymous Wars

The tensions in the Middle East or in Asia do not fully define today's risks to global political stability. Interstate tensions are nothing new, and the concerns over Iran and stability in Asia are not without historical precedent. What introduces a unique dimension of threat into the twenty-first century is rather the dangerous way that the evolution of cyber technology, drone sophistication, and terrorist networks are altering the basic norms within which states themselves interact. The result could be unprecedented anonymous wars.

The two centuries since the Congress of Vienna have seen the gradual codification by the international community of the "rules of the game" for guiding interstate relations, even between unfriendly countries. The basic premise has been the formula "don't do to me what you don't want me to do to you." However, technological advances mean that today those rules could be dangerously undermined. The international system is at risk.

After the age of Metternich, Talleyrand, and Castlereagh, elaborate understandings developed about the transition from formal peace to war. These involved carefully scripted exchanges of diplomats, rules about the treatment of prisoners of war, and eventually even a shared definition of war crimes. Implicit in all this was the notion that while war and peace are fundamentally different conditions, both still need rules of conduct. In more recent times, the use of nuclear weapons has made the distinction between the two more dramatic. The destructiveness of these weapons was without precedent but paradoxically that encouraged more cautious behavior on the part of the states that possessed them. The existence of such weapons also created a new global hierarchy with a few nuclear states at the top and the rest below.

Today, the interstate rules of the game are degrading. Highly sophisticated capabilities for inflicting violence on remote targets, as well as cross-border, state-sponsored terrorism, are undermining the clear demarcation of what is permissible and what is not. Scientific advances have also increased the potential scope of acts whose perpetrators may not be easily identified and that may not be intercepted in a timely fashion. Indeed, the world community is witnessing an increasing reliance by states on covert acts of violence without declarations of war. Leaders can now use long-distance air drones for lethal strikes across national borders against targeted individuals, occasionally killing civilians, too.

The sophisticated dissemination of computer viruses can disrupt the military-industrial assets of rivals. States can commission unacknowledged assassinations of foreign leaders and of scientists engaged in weapons development. They may back hacking of foreign institutions for intelligence purposes as well as of private business entities to gain commercial advantages. Some states are also experimenting with more comprehensive cyber warfare designed to disrupt the operational infrastructure of targeted states, as in the case of the assault on Estonia and its banking institutions in 2007. A rogue but technologically sophisticated state can now gain the capacity to launch a nonlethal but paralyzing cyber attack on the socioeconomic system and the most important state institutions of a target country without the source of the attack being promptly identifiable.

The dangers inherent in the degradation of the already-vulnerable international system cannot be overstated. Social chaos, with paralyzing fear magnified by uncertainty as to its origins, could spread. Making matters potentially even worse, such degradation is not the product of one or another particularly menacing state. Rather, it is the consequence of the rising vulnerability of the global system to cumulative pressures: technological innovation, massive and increasingly impatient populist upheavals, and a shift in the distribution of geopolitical power.

In that volatile context, competing states tend to be subjective in judgments of their own conduct. There are lessons here to be learned from the onset of the nuclear-weapons age. After the end of the Second World War in 1945, the United States wisely abstained from a preemptive attack on the USSR that would have exploited its atomic monopoly but that probably would have had monstrous consequences. But self-restraint ushered in a Soviet effort to gain, first, nuclear equality, and then superiority. America's admirably consistent determination to prevent the latter, as well as probably also the rise of a nuclear-armed but increasingly anti-Soviet China, compelled the Soviet Union to settle eventually for verifiable nuclear-weapons parity.

An open discussion of today's novel risks to global stability might still help to avert unprecedented disasters. Responsible governments with a stake in global stability and technological capacity need to convene a process designed to set rules that inhibit the drift towards covert acts of aggression. As the world's foremost innovator, the United States should take the lead. But to make that process productive, the United States itself—while resisting the temptation to do to others what America condemns others for doing—must make certain that its vulnerabilities are not easily exploited by adversaries who are difficult to identify. It is perplexing that the United States, which apparently is able to use computers to inject undetectable viruses into sensitive foreign targets, seems so vulnerable and so uninformed regarding foreign hacking into its own assets.

Calm and determined deterrence—including intensified efforts to identify perpetrators credibly as well as readiness to retaliate in kind—must be the point of departure for new and genuinely reciprocal rules of the game. The need for such rules is becoming urgent.

The twenty-first century may yet become an era of renewed prosperity for America's values and people. But in each instance, the key to success is avoiding a foolhardy rush toward simplistic and bellicose solutions at the expense of more sophisticated, measured, and principled responses. In these increasingly complex and interconnected times, hasty and unilateral solutions—often urged upon America by foreign interests—are no longer consistent with the spirit and realities of our new age. The great challenge today is not hegemony, but turmoil, and coping with the latter requires strategic vision, firmness of purpose, and a clear sense of our values.

ACKNOWLEDGMENTS

Writing a book is a lonely process, but an intellectually stimulating and congenial setting can make the task much easier. Likewise, the assistance of a professionally skillful staff can provide essential research backup and helpful suggestions while shielding the author from disruptive distractions. The publisher's editor, as the source of the first external appraisal of the significance and clarity of the author's message, can help to refine the manuscript into an actual book. And last but far from least in importance, a critically minded but sympathetic spouse can be the vital source both of blunt criticism and of occasionally badly needed encouragement. I was fortunate in all these respects, and I feel most grateful.

The CSIS, superbly headed now for more than a decade by John Hamre, provided countless opportunities for refining my geopolitical perspective on world affairs and on America's role in them. Similarly, SAIS of Johns Hopkins University gave me a platform for a critical dialogue with its faculty headed by its intellectually dynamic Dean Jessica Einhorn. One could not ask for a better combination. My office at CSIS—skillfully, reliably, and cheerfully managed by Diane Reed—kept me focused on the essentials and thus free of time-consuming distractions.

My two very gifted and energetic research assistants, Ted Bunzel and Matt King, both recruited from Yale University's demanding international affairs program, provided a talented testing ground for my "strategic vision" as well as vitally essential research support. More specifically, Ted, present at the book's inception, helped to refine my initial outline for the book and to assemble the supporting data, especially for the book's first half. He also helped to organize the critical socioeconomic analysis of US prospects in the book's Part II. Matt then took over, and in Part III he ably transformed my initial topical outline for the sections dealing with Mexico and the global commons into actual drafts for my review. He was creative in developing the maps and the charts for the second half of the book. In the concluding stages of our work, he played a truly vital role in helping me to tighten the entire manuscript, to refine its central argument, and also to respond to the many questions raised by the publisher's editor. Finally, he actively participated in the deliberations concerning the choice of the title for the book.

Tim Bartlett, the meticulous editor of Basic Books, was a challenging critic. He exposed weaknesses in my reasoning, he was relentless in drawing attention to my repetitions and thus helped to shape a leaner and more focused manuscript, he raised pointed questions regarding the broader historical canvas of the book's geopolitical argument, and he was constructively engaged in our discussions concerning the book's title. Credit is also due to others at Basic Books for their input: notably Michele Jacob, director of publicity; Kay Mariea, director of editor services; and Paula Cooper, copy editor. They all helped to make the book better and thus, I hope, more widely read.

As in the case of all of my books, my wife, Muska, was the essential source of personal encouragement. She pushed me to write it. She challenged me to persist. She read and ruthlessly dissected my initial drafts. She was as relentless in her constructive critiques as in her urging that I be bold in advocating a more promising strategic vision of tomorrow than merely a continuation of what is today.

NOTES

PART 1

1. Peter Nolan, *Crossroads* (London, 2009), 220. See also Daniel Yergin, *The Prize* (New York, 1993), 401.

2. World Bank: World Development Indicators, April 26, 2011.

3. Donald J. Puchala, "The History of the Future of International Relations," *Ethics and International Relations* 8 (1994): 197.

PART 2

1. James Thomson, *A House Divided* (Arlington, VA, 2010), 17.

PART 3

1. "China's Future Global Position," *Liaowang*, October 19, 2008.

2. "Competition and Cooperation Between China and the United States Are Intermingled," *Liaowang*, February 7, 2010.

3. "China's Expanding War Game," *Hindustan Times*, August 25, 2010.

4. Secretary of State Clinton, Joint Press Conference in Tbilisi, July 6, 2010.

5. As proposed in this writer's "A Plan for Europe," *Foreign Affairs*, January 1995.

6. *Mexican Immigrants: How Many Come? How Many Leave?* Pew Hispanic Center Report, July 22, 2009.

7. *Estimates of Unauthorized Immigrant Population Residing in the United States: January 2009*, Department of Homeland Security, Office of Immigration Statistics, January 2010, www.dhs.gov/xlibrary/assets/statistics/publications/ois_ill_pe_2009.pdf.

8. Clare Ribando Seelke, Mark P. Sullivan, and June S Beittel, *Mexico-US Relations: Issues for Congress*, Congressional Research Service, February 3, 2010.

9. *The Global Water Crisis*, USAID, January 18, 2007.

10. Vladimir Radyuhin, "The Arctic's Strategic Value for Russia," *The Hindu*, October 30, 2010, www.thehindu.com/opinion/lead/article857542.ece.

11. G. P. Glasby and Yu L. Voytekhovsky, "Arctic Russia: Minerals and Mineral Resources," *Geochemical News*, no. 140 (July 2009).

12. Radyuhin, "Arctic's Strategic Value."

PART 4

1. "Europe's Last Chance," *Korea Times*, October 13, 2010.

2. See a fuller explanation of this concept in this author's 2004 book *The Choice,* 59 and 79.

3. Giovanni Arrighi, *Adam Smith in Beijing: Lineages of the 21st Century* (London, 2007), 314–315.

4. "Over the Next 10 Years, Mass Incidents Will Be the Greatest Challenge to Governance," *Liaowang Dongfang Zhoukan,* April 21, 2010.

INDEX